THE RIDE OF YOUR LIFE

25 Reasons Why Theme Parks Are Modern Shrines

Michael Fridgen

ISBN: 978-0-9968574-4-4 (sc)
ISBN: 978-1-4834-9050-2 (e)

Library of Congress Control Number: 2018910178

Lulu Publishing Services rev. date: 09/12/2018

For Spencer

Contents

Introduction

During the famously nostalgic 1983 movie *A Christmas Story,* Ralphie's teacher gives the class of nine-years-olds the assignment to write a theme. The subject of this theme: "What I Want for Christmas." Here is what my nine-year-old self would have written—mistakes included for authenticity.

What I Want for Christmas

I want a ticket to Valleyfair for Christmas. Valleyfair is this amusement park in a town that I can't spell but its in Minnesota somewhere around the twin city's. This is a great idea for Chrismas.

Valleyfair has a white roller coaster that is called the high roller. Its good for a family to ride even if one of the kids throws up. There is also this thing that spins you around and it looks like you will hit someone else but you never will.

It is very good to go to Valleyfair when you want to practice to be a grown up because you can drive this old car around a track and over a bridge with your sisters in the back. I don't like it when my one sister wants to drive the car. She gets everything.

I don't think that mittens are a very good Chrismas present.

What do you think? Would I get the coveted A+++ or the more realistic C+? I realize that my grammar needs work, but what teacher could deny the assertion that a theme park ticket is a great gift for any occasion? (In addition, the chances of having your eye shot out at the theme park are extremely rare.) Regardless of what my teacher thought, I love theme parks and always have. And I'm not alone.

According to the Themed Entertainment Association report, in 2016, 438,267,000 people visited a park owned by one of the ten largest entertainment companies on the planet. Undeniably, these ten organizations control a major share of the amusement industry, but there are certainly thousands of parks not accounted for in this particular report. Nobody knows exactly; however, it's a fairly educated estimate to assume that in 2016 around one billion people visited some type of entertainment park. Now that's a lot of funnel cakes and Mickey ears.

If you want to impress people by throwing around a fancy word, here's one for you: *simulacrum.* I don't know the origin of the word except that it sounds like something Julius Caesar left on the table after eating a breakfast pastry. It's a word that professors of philosophy use. *Simulacrum* means, according to French sociologist Jean Baudrillard, "a façade, willingly embraced, that replaces actual experience with virtual experience and is often hermetically sealed." *Simulacrum* makes a nice (i.e. adequate) academic (i.e. stuffy) description of the places I love.

I have some issues with the concept of a simulacrum. Just

because something is virtual, does that make it any less actual? Hermetically sealing is what provides me with comfort, safety, and nostalgia—but does that mean that it's all a façade?

There is a famous story that is told in several biographies of Walt Disney. One day, Walt was giving a tour of Disneyland to a visiting celebrity—as one does when one owns a theme park. Upon leaving the park, the celebrity stopped and said, "Well, Walt, you got a nice fantasy here."

Walt was quick to respond, "Oh, no, you are mistaken. Disneyland is not a fantasy and is very real. Inside this park, people are nice to each other. They have fun and watch out for the wellbeing of children. The people inside Disneyland smile at each other and laugh. They imagine what it was like to be part of an old town, or a royal dignitary in a castle, or an astronaut orbiting the earth. But outside these gates, people hurt each other. They hate and scowl—that's the fantasy because it's not who we are and what we should be. Disneyland is the reality."

It's my hope that after you read this book, you will agree with Walt and reject the thoughts of façades with hermetically sealed fake realities. Here, I will present twenty-five reasons why theme parks are among the most important places on the planet. More than a destination, project, or business, theme parks are part of the human experience. As long as we need to have fun (and, wow, more than ever we surely need to have fun), we will need theme parks.

What Is a Theme Park?

All that talk of humanity and being nice didn't last long. I'm about to offer a divisive topic: What is a theme park? Well, the answer isn't as simple as you may think, and like with everything else, opinions on the matter differ.

The noun *theme park* is fairly modern and didn't attain wide usage until the mid-1990s. In fact, there are still entire generations that use *amusement park* because historically, that's the term that stuck. There are countless other names, among them these: *fun zone, midway, carnival, arcade,* and *living history park.* A newer term, *iron park,* is used by enthusiasts to describe parks that place more emphasis on extreme rides and less emphasis on theming. To complicate matters, the Walt Disney Company insists that its creations are a whole different experience called *Disney Parks.* (Yes, with a capital D and P.) And we all have that grumpy uncle who uses *waste of money* as a noun for these places.

Among all the bickering, most people can agree that the *park* of *theme park* and *amusement park* came first. Since the beginning of organized community living, humans have set aside places to play. More than likely, parks were created because some cave parents got tired of their cave children driving them nuts. They told them to go and smash rocks together with some other cave kids in that faraway field where nobody could hear them—that was the first park. After the cave kids went to their stone beds, the cave adults wanted to hang out, and they also went to the faraway field—this was the first Pleasure Island.

As time went on, some of these parks added equipment to help make the fun more fun. Thus, *amusement park* became the title of choice for these places. However, by the mid-twentieth century, the term *amusement park* carried negative connotations: they were dirty places that employed criminals and used shady business practices. In order to separate themselves from the bad seeds, some parks embraced a concept that unified the guests' experiences. These concepts, or themes, led to the preferred noun of *theme park.*

Even though some parks contain attractions but do not have a central theme, we still call them theme parks. Most parks of the Six Flags and Cedar Fair organizations do not have themes; however, using the term *amusement park* to describe them just doesn't sound right. Am I telling you that this whole theme park deal is all semantics without a proper definition? Yep, that's exactly what I'm telling you.

Now that we've settled on a name, what exactly are theme parks? Well, theme parks are parks that have rides—except when they don't. They are places that have a single entry and one cost of admission—except when they don't. Theme parks are large entertainment zones with food and merchandise—except when they're not. You see, theme parks come in all shapes and sizes—that's part of what makes them so great.

But, I understand that I have to present at least a working definition so that you will know what the heck I'm writing about. **To me, a theme park is a permanent geographic location of unspecified size that is open at least 120 days annually and serves the purpose of providing entertainment for humans.**

My definition excludes fairs due to their short length. I also don't include transitory carnivals. What about the collection of really crappy coin-operated kids' rides outside the grocery store? Believe it or not, that fits my definition.

A theme park has to be a place that you can experience time and time again. It has to be geographically permanent to give the visitor a sense of home. Theme parks are places where people can return to escape the world—that's why, for me, they have to be open for enough weeks that a multitude of people can find their escape.

I used the word *entertainment* in my definition. That word sounds a bit trivial, but please know that it is the most important word in my statement. Theme parks are places where people have fun, and there is absolutely nothing trivial about that. We need fun as much as we need food. There are those that believe they are too busy and productive to have fun—they should stay clear of me. I have no patience or pity for people who are too busy to enjoy the one life they will ever have.

What Is a Shrine?

Let me get this off my chest: I mean no disrespect for any religion or spirituality with my use of the world *shrine*. I am merely using the word to explain the importance that theme parks have come to have in my own life. Theme parks offer a spiritual experience for me. With that said, I'm quite accustomed to the normal religious definition of *shrine*.

I grew up in a very Catholic family in the middle of Minnesota. In Catholic heritage, a shrine is a place that has a portrait and/or statue of the Virgin Mary. (That's probably not the official definition from the Vatican, but like most Catholics of the 1970s, we didn't much care what was official. Instead, we gravitated toward the legendary, macabre, and downright weird things of Catholicism.)

We had a shrine in our backyard. My mom placed a two-foot-tall statue of the Virgin Mary between two trees that were growing out of one stump. Mary was standing on a snake, which always freaked me out, and I rarely went near the thing. The snake-crushing Virgin was meant to protect us from … well, I'm not sure what. Nothing really bad happened to us, so it must have worked. I guess, for me, the shrine was a creepy statue that may or may not have kept our home from burning down. However, for my mom, the shrine was an escape—it was a place she could visit that would take away her daily worries for a bit. She may have only visited the Madonna for short periods of time, but those were the moments when she could think and relax. (FYI: Madonna is what good Catholics call the Virgin Mary. My mom did not have a shrine to the Material Girl in our yard.)

As you'll learn in the next section of this book, I didn't grow up going to theme parks. In fact, our family travels revolved largely around shrines. Each summer, my sisters and I packed into the station wagon to visit the Our Lady of Something shrine in a God-knows-where midwestern small town. Again, for my parents it was all about escape. Shrines offered a place and time where they could pause and relax. (We kids were always well behaved at the shrines. It's hard to be a brat when literally facing the wrath of hell in the form of a giant flaming saint.) Actually, there was a great purpose for us children to visit shrines, as we learned to shut up, get along, occupy our time between hotel swimming pools, and generally grow up.

We still visit shrines. Last summer, I brought my eleven-year-old niece along as I took my ninety-eight-year-old grandma to Our Lady of Seven Dolars. (No, that's not a typo—and the Virgin is worth way more than seven dollars. A *dolar* is a time when Mary felt sorrow, like the time that Jesus broke a lamp while playing ball in the house.) As we were walking around the shrine, my niece said, "For Great-Grandma Francie, going to Our Lady of Seven Dolars is the same as me going to Disneyland." And that's how the idea for this book was born!

Shrines are not reserved only for Catholics. My husband and I love Japan (more on the unbelievable Tokyo Disney Resort later in this book). In Japan, beautiful shrines are seemingly all over. Even though the Shinto religion is not practiced in the same way it was prior to World War Two, shrines continue to play an important role in all of life's moments. Japanese shrines are where people grow up, get married, relax, reflect, escape, and finally move on to that big shrine in the sky.

As I mentioned earlier, I mean no disrespect in comparing theme parks to shrines. Theme parks really are that important to me. I've seen my nephews and niece grow up at theme parks; I've seen my grandparents grow old at them. I've had many moments of escape. The older I get, the more my moments of escape become moments of nostalgia. I see life inside theme parks the same way that many Japanese people see life inside the beautiful floating shrine outside Hiroshima. I don't think the nuns at Our Lady of Seven Dolars would approve of my theme park philosophy. But then, they aren't able to see inside my heart when the fireworks explode at Disneyland. If they could see inside my heart, they would know that I am happy and full of life at my shrine.

Consider the Source

In this age of Wikipedia and corporate publishing, it is important to carefully consider the author's expertise, especially while reading a book about travel. Teams of people assigned through a publisher write many bestselling guides and tour books. Sometimes these writers have not even visited the places they are offering advice about. So if you're wondering who wrote this book and why you should read it, I'm about to tell you. If you are not wondering or are anxious to get to the details, go ahead and skip to the next section.

When I was five years old, I received a map of Disney World's Magic Kingdom for Christmas. Today, if a kid gets a map of Disney World as a present, he or she can probably assume that the real gift is an actual trip to the famous park. But I knew that my family did not have the means to make such a journey. I also knew that my parents realized how much I loved looking at maps. Regardless, I can credit my many hours of staring at that map, and using it to drive my Matchbox cars on, as the beginning of my love of theme parks.

I liked maps of real places too, but these were usually messy, with mountains, rivers, and lakes to navigate. The Magic Kingdom map was beautifully drawn and instantly made sense to me. I took my little car and easily planned how to get from the entrance gate to the moat around Cinderella Castle. Many nights, I dreamed that someday I would spend one day at that magical place. But back then, I had no idea how my life would develop, and I couldn't imagine the numerous theme park visits I would one day make.

I grew up in Minnesota, and every year we took the two-hour journey by station wagon to spend one day at what I thought was the happiest place on earth: Valleyfair in Shakopee, Minnesota. I vividly remember getting little sleep the night before because of all the anticipation. I also remember saying a prayer because I was afraid that if our house burned down during the night, we wouldn't be able to go there.

They called Valleyfair a theme park, but even today, I'm unsure what the theme was. Back then, a large, patriotic man called Colonel John Phillips Oom-pa-pa roamed the asphalt with his girlfriend, Chocolate Moose. She was a furry brown moose that wore a frilly dress and straw hat; I always thought she looked like Minnie Pearl from the television show *Hee Haw*. Valleyfair had these ladybugs that went around in a circle and an enormous green chair where the Jolly Green Giant supposedly sat, although we never saw him.

I'm unsure how that one glorious day each summer and my Disney World map turned into a lifelong obsession with theme parks. I'd probably need to employ a psychiatrist with deep analytical skills to determine what from my childhood made me crave the fantasy realness of a themed land. But when it comes down to it, I guess I don't care why or how I got this way because it's a good way to be. Hey, there are a lot of other worse obsessions I could have.

I believe that theme parks are truly magical places because they force us to forget the real world and pause for reflection.

Each year, it's where we kids measured our progress toward adulthood. Nothing marks time better than the ride attendant holding up a painted wood pole next to you and stating that you can go on the High Roller. That pole measured both our physical growth and inner bravery. Every summer, our parents saw the changes in us, and we saw the difference in ourselves. I didn't grow up in the age of box socials and cotillions. Our annual trip to Valleyfair is how we Generation Xers marked time.

I was twenty-one years old the first time I stepped foot inside a Disney Park. (Yep, I was a late bloomer.) My parents, sister, grandparents, and I drove from central Minnesota to Orlando. We didn't have many resources at the time, and we packed all of our food into a small trailer that we pulled behind our vehicle. We stayed, all of us in one room, at a motel in Kissimmee, Florida. I'm not sure which motel it was, but I think the name was something like the Cockroach/Drug Dealer/Mass Murderer Motel. (Thankfully, the budget hotel market has improved greatly in the past twenty years. There are now many options that are safer and cleaner. Even Disney offers several value choices in Orlando.)

I was beyond excited. Remember, I'd had a map of the place since I was five. But, alas, sometimes travel throws you a curve. Even though Orlando is in Florida, it is very rare for a hurricane to directly impact the area. Walt Disney World is in the central part of the Florida peninsula; hurricanes tend to hit the coasts and the southern tip. Regardless, in 1995, Hurricane Erin hit the Murder Motel the first night of our arrival. This storm crossed the entire peninsula, hitting both coasts, Orlando, and the panhandle. It was windy. And rainy. And thundering. And very, very windy. Seriously, it was windy.

The next morning, there was no electricity in the motel, and most of the windows had been broken. The worst news, as heard on our emergency travel radio, was that the Disney theme parks were temporarily closed. I was heartbroken. My grandma got bored and decided to wash all our clothes in the bathtub. (Yes, we really were that cheap.) She didn't figure that the electricity would be out for days, rendering the motel dryers useless. So Grandpa, in all his Depression-era glory, got some rope from our food trailer and strung up our wet underwear between a couple of palm trees. And then, in the middle of the afternoon, the Blue Fairy must have heard my wish. The radio announced that the Magic Kingdom was open!

We left our hanging clothes, thinking that drug dealers had more money than us and probably wouldn't want anything we had. Orlando was a mess of branches, paper, and yard furniture. We doubted the radio's news of an open Magic Kingdom when we saw that nobody in the city had any power. But then we took an exit off the highway and saw our first Disney road signs. They had their own road signs! I jumped out of my skin.

Believe it or not, the sun was shining. The entire Walt Disney Resort had electricity because they make their own and channel it underground. I saw the gates—those wonderful, magical gates that still send a shiver through my body. My nineteen-year-old sister screamed with joy. At that moment, we weren't hurricane-ravaged adults carrying our own food from the Murder Motel, where our underwear currently hung. Magically, we were all kids.

I remember each detail of that wonderful afternoon and evening: the monorail, the castle, ghosts, pirates, country bears, presidents, happy dolls, Donald Duck. I grasped as much of it as I could because I thought I'd probably never travel back there. I bought a Mickey Mouse mug. Little did I know the kind of life that I would have one day.

Through some smart decisions and hard work, I've obtained a life where I am fortunate enough to be able to travel to the places I love. I've been to many theme parks in the United States and abroad. I've been multiple times to each of the Disney parks around the globe. I count among my favorite places Dollywood in Tennessee, Ocean Park in Hong Kong, Tivoli Gardens in Copenhagen, Europa-Park in Germany, and DisneySea in Tokyo.

All of us take many roles in life. In order for any one place to be considered a true lifelong destination, it must be able to appeal to you during all those changing roles. Theme parks have not disappointed me in this regard. As my own life has changed, I've experienced theme parks in new and different ways.

I have been to theme parks as

- a small kid being pushed around by his parents
- a preteen trying to be brave with friends
- a high schooler on a marching band trip
- a college student traveling with family
- a working adult traveling with family
- an uncle with a ten-month-old nephew
- a grandson with elderly grandparents
- a single person who just wanted to get away
- an adult traveling with other adult friends whom I coerced into going
- an uncle with preteen and toddler nephews
- part of a couple on our honeymoon
- a person in a wheelchair after having ankle surgery
- an uncle with a teenage nephew, preteen nephew, and a third kid, my niece
- part of a couple still choosing to spend vacation time in a fantasy realness

In the 1970s, my grandma chased after me at Valleyfair when I wanted to ride the little boats instead of eating. Thirty years later, I ran around that same park trying to find which shop she had gone to. I hope in thirty more years my nephews and niece will be able to push me around the attractions as I now push them around the play areas.

And that brings me back to my original point: Theme parks are magical places because they give us pause to mark the progress we make as people. It's my hope that you will travel to your own Valleyfair and use the fantasy realness to mark your own life. Mostly, I hope you've learned from this section that you can trust me to write this book.

Developing a Theme Park Philosophy

I've heard this strange rumor that some people don't like theme parks. I've met some of these people. Some of them are even productive, law-abiding citizens.

All kidding aside, when I ask people why they didn't have a magical time on their theme park vacation, it's usually because they pursued a side of theme parks that didn't meet their purpose. One of my colleagues wanted a relaxing time creating memories with her kids. She chose the Walt Disney World Resort in Florida as her destination. However, while at the Magic Kingdom, she wanted everyone to see everything. Consequently, her family drove each other nuts as they forced themselves to run through each park for days. Another couple I know desired a very active theme park vacation and was dismayed when they had to spend a lot of time stuck in traffic. They all came away hating theme parks—but that wasn't the theme park industry's fault.

My colleague made the mistake of forcing activity when so many lovely Disney pools would have been better. The couple I mentioned made the mistake of not staying at a hotel close to the theme parks. But in both cases, they made the crucial mistake of traveling without a philosophy. We don't often ask ourselves, "Why do I want to travel, and how can my destination support that purpose?"

I have a good friend who knows that in addition to theme parks, I also love Las Vegas. (I guess Las Vegas is kind of like one big theme park for adults.) One winter, she thought she'd vacation in Sin City. She hated it and wasn't afraid to share that with me. "Everything was so fake—not just the buildings, but also the people. Everything is about money there, and I just couldn't stand all the superficial people running around. The whole town was about status, money, and how trashy you could look."

Now I know what some of you are thinking: "What in the world was she expecting? What did she think Las Vegas was—a Tibetan monastery?" Well, in this case, the destination was not the problem. The destination is rarely the problem. The problem was that my friend didn't consider what kind of experience she wanted on vacation. Why did she want to travel, and how could Las Vegas support that purpose?

There are plenty of authentic experiences to be had in Las Vegas. She could have visited the superb cactus gardens at Ethel M's Chocolate Factory. Both Grand Canyon and Zion national parks are easy drives away. A tour of Zappo's corporate headquarters gives great insight into the workings of a socially responsible company. The Neon Graveyard is fascinating from both a historical and design perspective.

My friend fell into the trap of doing what she thought she had to do in Las Vegas. She was stuck in casinos on the Strip because that's the Las Vegas she saw on television. She should have crafted a more tailored itinerary. However, this is easier said than done due to societal pressure.

As soon as you tell someone that you're going to Las Vegas, you will get all sorts of advice and stories about how to go crazy on Las Vegas Boulevard. You'll hear all about the hotels and bars that you must go to because so and so had an epic night there. When you return home, it gets even worse. You will have to face the barrage of "Did you see that? No? Oh, you really missed out." My advice: Don't let other people's expectations of your trip have an impact on your journey.

When it becomes known that your family has chosen a Disney vacation, former Disney travelers will come out of the wood-work. They will each have a list of things you must do or else your trip will not be nearly as good as theirs was. There are also 12,258 blogs telling you how to vacation with Disney. Of course, it's fine to seek guidance and learn from others who have experience. But again, don't let other people's expectations of your trip have an impact on your journey.

I've been on trips to Walt Disney World when I've never set foot in a theme park. This may sound very strange, but it's true. The Disney resorts in Florida are huge, with lots of activities and amenities. Outside of the resorts, Disney Springs is an en-tertainment district that is as large as a theme park and doesn't require any admission to enter. There are watercraft activities on Disney's Bay Lake and the Seven Seas Lagoon. Sometimes this is the kind of vacation that I want.

To develop a theme park philosophy, you need to filter through a lot of information. Filter out whatever the theme park marketers are promoting—they have an ulterior motive to offer you what they think you want to experience (i.e. purchase). Sort and filter the suggestions you get from others who have vis-ited your theme park destination before—they may have good experience, but you don't need to recreate their memorable journey. Resist the temptation to follow bloggers with lists of attractions you can't miss. In fact, I run away whenever I see the term *must-do.* When I vacation at a theme park, there is nothing I must do—only what I want to do.

On the opening day of his theme park, Walt Disney famously said, "Disneyland is your land." That's how you should approach any theme park. It's your money and it's your time—spend it the way you want.

To summarize this section, remember these three things:

- Spend some time before your departure considering what kind of experience you want to have on vacation.
- Take advice from others, but don't let them dictate your journey.
- It's okay to do things that are not typical for your destination.

So go ahead and vacation the way you want. After all, it's your time and money. I'm giving you permission to go to Hawaii and skip the beach. Go to Rome and pass on the pasta. Go to Japan and eat at McDonald's. Go to Disneyland and sleep in, or get up early because you love theme parks in the morning, or avoid the park and spend the day by the pool. Be brave, and don't ever be ashamed to enjoy life the way you want to enjoy it.

Dreamlly's Theme Park Recommendation

This is Dreamlly; he is a narwhal. I love narwhals because none have ever survived in captivity. A few of them have been caught, but they always manage to die shortly after being confined. Yeah,

I know it all sounds a bit morbid—but I like the fact that they'd rather die than be captive for life. The name Dreamlly is a conglomeration of one of my favorite places with one of my favorite people. *Dream* is from the Disney Dream cruise ship—a theme park at sea. The *lly* is from Dolly, as in Dolly Parton—a musical genius that has her own theme park (in my opinion, she has reached the absolute height of human achievement).

Dreamlly is going to show up at the conclusion of each of the twenty-five reasons why theme parks are modern shrines. He's going to present a park that exemplifies whatever reason is being explained. It's Dreamlly's hope that he'll inspire you to visit at least a few of the wonderful theme parks he describes.

Reason #1:

While literally measuring the process of aging, theme parks are all about growing up.

Unlike most kids, I never wanted to grow up and become an adult. Somehow, I've always known the adults had to work hard and deal with problems. But ironically, I desperately wanted to be physically taller. When I was a kid, Valleyfair had this beat-up old wooden pole to measure height. The coaster attendant wielded the pole with the power of Thor. At one point, the pole had been painted bright red with a black stripe. That stripe was exactly forty-four inches from the bottom. However, by the time I was tall enough to be considered pole-worthy, it had faded to a shade of pink, and the black stripe had been reinforced several times with a crude Sharpie marker.

Thor had the pole, and my destiny was in his hands. In reality, he was likely a sixteen-year-old B honor roll student at Shakopee High School. But to me, he was a Norse god who held the power of fun within his grasp. There was a height measure located near the entrance to the ride, but it would have been unwise to place any trust in that inferior device because Thor's pole had the final word.

Even though it sometimes seems like we are still just animals fighting each other in the wild, we have managed some progress as a species. Our children can now develop and mature before we send them into the workforce—or slavery—or marriage—or all of the above. No longer do young boys have to hear, "Well, Ezekiel, you're taller than the milk jug, and that means you're going to fight the Ottoman Empire." And young girls don't wake up to "Git out of bed, Sarah Jane. Yer gonna take a bath in the creek. Yep, I know you went an' had a bath jest a month ago, but today's yer weddin' day. Yer new husband, Old Man McCreepy, is a-waitin' fer ya out by the glade."

Thankfully, we've come a long way. But a question remains: How do we measure growth and development? Due to their inherent need to offer something for everyone, theme parks are a one-stop shop of developmentally appropriate experiences. (As a side note, Walt Disney World in Florida offers a perk for the not-quite-tall-enough. If, after waiting in line, you're still not tall enough to ride one of the thrill rides, you will be handed a small card. The card enables you to ride the attraction without waiting in line once you've grown that extra inch. When you are tall enough, just use the FastPass+ lane and avoid the regular queue. The back of the card becomes a small certificate of achievement that the ride attendant will complete for you!)

Before I faced Thor's pole, when I was still terrified of even a kiddie coaster, I loved those cop cars that went around in a small circle at Valleyfair. I was careful to steer my little cop car around the circle—I certainly did not want to crash into another vehicle and embarrass myself. I was too stupid to notice that each car was attached to the rotating center mechanism. Worse than that, I was too stupid to notice that the kid right next to me, in the same car, also had his own steering wheel.

I don't remember when I was too old for the little cop cars. I just remember one horrible summer when I thought that Valleyfair had nothing for me to do. This was before the age of family coasters and the realization that tweens were a viable market. And so the fact was clear: I had to either grow taller than Thor's pole or sit next to my Grandma Francie in front of the Gazebo Stage for a show called *In the Mood: Let's All Enjoy Every Song from the 1940s While the Taller Kids Are Riding the Coasters.*

Then, one glorious day in the mid '80s, my friend Chuck and I faced Thor during a middle school band trip. I was timid and scared, but I marched right up to that sixteen-year-old god and stared at the pole. Thor grabbed the pole and held it against my side. I was frozen with fear and didn't want to move, but I just had to know. I turned my head slightly and strained to make my eyeball rotate as far as it could. That's when I saw it: the black stripe! If I could see the black stripe, then I knew that I was tall enough. Oddly, though, my first thought wasn't one of joy. It was *Jeez, that pole is dirty. I think I just got a sliver in my ear.*

You may think that the story ends here—with Chuck and me screaming our heads off and then laughing insanely and running back into the line. But the truth is, I didn't stop growing up just because I'd conquered the pole. Interestingly, theme parks have been there every step of the way.

After thirty years of riding any coaster I encountered, one day I got just a bit sick. It wasn't a big deal, and I dealt with it—until the day that I couldn't. Apparently, I'd grown into another phase when turning upside down wasn't fun. Ironically, I'd entered a phase when seeing a theme park show became incredibly fun.

I'd also discovered that watching others on a roller coaster is way more fun than I'd ever imagined.

Not too long ago, I noticed that theme parks have benches! I use them from time to time. Oh, I'm not ready to hand over my season pass yet. I'm still game for any non-inverting coaster. But I see the appeal of the shows ... and parades ... and flowers ... and carousels ... and food that takes longer than thirty seconds to prepare.

I still feel like I don't want to grow up. But oddly, I also hope that I never stop growing. Someday, you may see a very old man sitting on a bench at Dollywood or Disneyland or some theme park that is still inside a dreamer's mind. That old man will be eating popcorn—I love popcorn.

Dreamlly's Theme Park Recommendation

Knott's Berry Farm
Buena Park, California

Knott's Berry Farm is one of the two theme parks that claim to be America's first—more on that later. I chose Knott's to represent reason #1 because it contains attractions for all ages, from an awesome children's land to amazing coasters.

Knott's Berry Farm is located in Buena Park, California, about twenty-five miles east of Los Angeles International Airport and just a stone's throw from Anaheim. In fact, there are rooms on the upper floors of the Disneyland Hotel that have a better view of Knott's than they do of Disneyland itself!

Camp Snoopy, Knott's children's land, is considered by most theme park enthusiasts as the best kid-centered area of any park in the US. The theming is incredibly well-done, and Camp Snoopy is a great stop for any fan of Snoopy, Charlie Brown, and the rest of the Peanuts gang. Just the Camp Snoopy land alone occupies six full acres.

When the kids grow up, they can try one of nine roller coasters. HangTime is the only dive coaster on the west coast of the United States. Knott's is home to GhostRider, the longest wooden coaster in California—it contains almost one mile of track. The park also has a drop tower, rotating extreme swing, and several other thrill rides. As much as I love Disneyland, I admit that thrill seekers will prefer Knott's collection of rides. (If your family is visiting Disneyland and you have some cranky teenagers along, just send them in an Uber over to Buena Park. It's only six miles away.)

One of the unique, and best, theme park shows I've ever seen is Mystery Lodge. After waiting in a beautiful and highly themed preshow area, guests are escorted into a traditional longhouse to meet a storyteller. The storyteller presents the traditions of the Kwak'wala, a group of indigenous people of the Pacific Northwest. While performing around a fire, the storyteller uses his hands to produce shapes out of the smoke. There isn't a consensus among fans as to how the effect is produced—and Knott's has never disclosed the technology. Some say Mystery Lodge uses reflections on glass; others say it's done with holograms. I think it's a combination of both. Regardless, the experience is amazing, and it blows my mind that this show opened in 1994.

I get frustrated when I see bad audience behavior at theme

park shows (seriously, people, thirty minutes is not too long to shut up). However, I've rarely seen bad behavior at Mystery Lodge. The show is so captivating that even the most jaded of tweens put down their phones and stare at the storyteller's hands in amazement.

The Ghost Town land of Knott's Berry Farm is the best themed section of the park. Way back when, Mr. Knott opened a street recreated from the old West so that diners at his wife's restaurant had something to do while they waited. He soon added a train that is still in use today. Yes, Mrs. Knott's Restaurant is also still in operation. The famous recipe for Mrs. Knott's fried chicken is secret and has not changed since 1934.

Before the restaurant opened in 1934, Mr. Knott ran a berry stand on this location in 1920. The berry portion of the Knott's empire was sold to Smucker's in the 1990s. However, jams and jellies bearing Knott's name can still be purchased in the park. No visit to Knott's Berry Farm would be complete without a sample of Knott's Boysenberry Punch.

In 1932, Mr. Knott tracked down the mythical berry after hearing about a rogue farmer experimenting on a farm in Northern California. But farmer Rudolph Boysen had given up and sold his farm. Mr. Knott actually crawled around the abandoned farm and found one dying bush among the weeds. He brought the bush back to Knott's Berry Farm, nursed it, and named the delicious fruit *boysenberry* after its creator. The boysenberry is a cross between raspberry, blackberry, dewberry, and loganberry.

Guests can eat at Mrs. Knott's Restaurant and enjoy the boysenberry punch without paying park admission. The restaurant and its attached California Marketplace are open to the public. Quite near Mrs. Knott's Restaurant is an exact replica of Independence Hall. And, I mean exact. The Knotts had seen the building on a trip to Philadelphia and obtained the original blueprints. They wanted students on the west coast to be able to view the birthplace of America. They built their replica of Independence Hall to the exact specifications of the blueprints, even chemically replicating the paint.

Due to its importance as a national monument, the real Independence Hall in Philadelphia does not allow interior filming. If you've seen a movie that showed the inside of Independence Hall, including *National Treasure* with Nicholas Cage, it was actually filmed at Knott's Berry Farm. Guests can tour Knott's Independence Hall without paying for theme park admission. And if you tell the parking attendant that you are there just to visit Independence Hall, they will allow you to park for free.

Knott's Berry Farm includes a full water park and hotel on its property. The water park does have separate admission. Knott's Berry Farm Hotel has rooms that are themed after Snoopy and Woodstock. They are adorable and can be booked online. There are even packages that include a bedtime visit from Snoopy himself!

Knott's Berry Farm is part of the true Southern California theme park experience. It's full of history, rides for all ages, and really good food. Everyone, from very young children to very young children at heart, can find something to do at Knott's.

Reason #2:

Theme parks are full of history

It's quite difficult to pinpoint the exact moment when the first theme park was created. In fact, if you ask several theme park enthusiasts about the first theme park, you will get several different answers. (Be advised: Don't ask this question if several theme park fans are in the same room—an argument of epic proportion will erupt, and you may not survive the fallout. Plus, blood is hard to get out of the carpet.)

We know that the ancient Persian king Xerxes began an annual exposition around 486 BC. These expositions were yearly gatherings of merchants, farmers, and nobility. While these events included a combination of education, commerce, and leisure, they weren't permanent and were certainly not themed (unless the theme was ancient Persian festival). King Xerxes's expositions were more similar to the concept of a world's fair than they were to modern theme parks. Honestly, they probably didn't even sell T-shirts at these things.

I like to believe that the first theme park was opened by Marie Antoinette in 1780. You may think I'm making another joke, but this time, I'm serious. If you don't believe me, you can go to Paris and see it for yourself.

Marie Antionette was born to the Hapsburg dynasty of Austria. She grew up at the family's country estate, Schönbrunn, just outside of Vienna. Little Marie had a beautiful childhood full of palatial opulence mixed with the barnyard animals that ran around the lawn.

In May of 1770, Marie Antoinette was married to the dauphin (crown prince) of France. This was a political and arranged marriage—the happy couple didn't meet until a few days before the wedding. Poor Marie was whisked away from her happy childhood and set into the virtual prison of the Versailles Palace in France. The court of Versailles was considerably more regimented than what Marie had experienced at Schönbrunn. Here, she had no freedom, and her every move was scrutinized.

What in the world does this have to do with theme parks? Well, after ten years of royal obedience and fulfilling her obligation of giving birth to a son, Marie Antoinette's husband, who was now King Louis XVI, gave her the funds to build a piece of Austria in France. Marie Antoinette, recently crowned Queen of France, designed and constructed the cutest themed land in history. The Hamlet of Marie Antionette was landscaped to replicate the countryside surrounding Vienna. Several structures were painstakingly created to capture the atmosphere of a charming countryside village.

Marie loved her Hamlet. She spent most days there, dressed as an Austrian farm maiden. In fact, all the servants of the Hamlet had costumes for their various roles. Animals were imported from Austria, and real crops were grown and harvested. Then, in the first theme park expansion in history, the Queen had the fantastical idea of building a theater.

Marie Antoinette loved the performing arts and was quite an actress herself. She built a small but opulent theater at her

Hamlet. The interior of the 250-seat theater looked like a miniature version of any of the grand opera houses of Europe. Because
she demanded quality, and because she had unlimited funds,
the Queen's theater included the most modern stage of its day.
Detailed sets were raised and lower using a system of winches
that were located in the attic. But to me, the most impressive
detail is that Marie hid all this from view. You see, it just simply
wouldn't do to have an opulent theater in the middle of a small
village. Instead, the entire structure is hidden behind large trees
that blend into the surrounding scene. Only a simple door can be
seen from the Hamlet itself.

Remember, all of this was accomplished exactly 175 years before Walt Disney hid his massive shops behind the ornate facades
of Main Street, USA. And, even more unbelievable, the Hamlet
survived not only the French Revolution but two world wars. You
can visit this themed and permanent park today on the grounds
of the Versailles Palace. They give out free cake. (Okay, that was
a joke.)

The history of theme parks is so exciting and vast that I've
broken it into three sections. Stay tuned for the birth of the
European amusement industry, the modern world's fair, and the
beginnings of theme parks as we know them today.

Dreamlly's Theme Park Recommendation

Marie Antionette's Hamlet
Versailles, France

This Dreamlly's park recommendation is, of course, Marie Antoinette's Hamlet. There aren't any roller coasters or funnel cakes, but there are attractions and the lavish theater. I've already described most of the details, but here is some helpful information if you plan to visit.

The Palace of Versailles is easily reached by train from Paris. Staff at any Paris hotel can help you find the correct regional train to the village of Versailles. The palace is a quick walk from the village station, and there are signs to point the way. In French, the word for *palace* is *chateau*.

Technically, you can visit the Hamlet without purchasing admission into the palace. However, I highly suggest that if you've made it all the way to Versailles, you spend the eighteen euros to see this magnificent structure. After your interior tour, you can wonder around the vast gardens and public spaces at your own pace. The Hamlet is well marked on all Versailles maps.

A bit of a walk through the famous gardens of Versailles is required. You'll know you're in the right place when you spot the most idyllic pond you've ever seen surrounded by several themed structures. Remember, none of the Hamlet was ever a real Austrian village and working farm—all of this was created to provide an escape for the Queen of France. Spend as much time as you can spare wandering around. Try to imagine the places where Marie and her children would pretend to be poor country farmers during a simpler time.

During most open hours, you can also step inside the very themed theater where Marie Antionette performed for her husband and the royal court of Versailles. Notice how the color and décor of the space were purposefully chosen to reflect the provincial feel of the Hamlet outside. Yes, it's opulent, but not in the same way as the grand opera house in Paris. This is the subdued, yet charming, opulence of a people who desperately wanted to forget everything happening in the real world.

The Hamlet continues to be stocked with Austrian animals, and you will even find that employees still dress in traditional clothes as they lovingly care for the village. The Hamlet embodies the human desire to recreate an atmosphere that inspires our imagination to help us relax and enjoy life. Just take a hint from Marie Antoinette's life: Theme parks are great places to visit for a temporary escape, but ignoring the real world for too long may impair your ability to relate to others.

Reason #3:

Theme parks offer a safe space to rehearse being a functioning member of society.

Imagine that you are the band teacher at Kennedy Middle School in Small Town, Illinois. The sixty students of your sixth-grade band started the school year by being real pains in the butt, as sixth graders are often known to be. But you, as a quality human and excellent teacher, decide not to give up on them. Instead, you devise a reward system based on points, with a field trip as the ultimate prize. Somehow, the sixth graders managed to pull their crap together, and by May, they'd earned the field trip.

And so, one fine day in early June, you load all sixty of them on a school bus and drive to the corner of Michigan and Monroe in the center of Chicago. As the kids get off the bus, you tell them, "All right, everyone, go wherever you want unchaperoned with your friends. I'll see you right back here in twelve hours. Don't be late."

Does dropping them off for twelve unsupervised hours in Chicago sound like a good idea? Of course not! This sounds like a good way to win Worst Teacher of the Year and maybe even face criminal charges. However, sixth-grade band teachers routinely allow their students to explore Six Flags Great America without chaperones.

There's quite a difference between downtown Chicago and Six Flags Great America—and it's more than just the forty-six miles that separate them. It's also the hidden magic of design and security that theme parks use to protect their guests and their own assets.

Sixth graders can wander unchaperoned inside a theme park because it's a faux society. Just like in the real world, theme parks have restaurants, shops, pedestrians, employees, money, and weather. The "faux" part, or what I prefer to call the "fantasy realness," lies with the entrance gate. There is a level of structure and seclusion inside a theme park that allows guests the ability to enjoy a functioning society without all the risks that sometimes occur in civilization.

Do all the sixth graders at Six Flags have a perfect, stress-free day? Of course not. Some of them get sick on rides, and others starve because they spent all their money on a basketball shooting game. One kid left her backpack outside a hotdog stand, and another had his wallet taken when he left his jacket unaccompanied while he used the restroom.

However, in this controlled environment, their lives weren't ruined. Yes, some had to contact park security and locate the lost and found office. Some had to go hungry, and that one kid faced the anger of losing the thirty dollars he had in his wallet. A few even had to locate the first aid building for Band-Aids. But think about what they gained—the ability to make their own decisions and mistakes without the direct watchful eyes of adults.

Beyond how to deal with their mistakes, the sixth graders also learned how to get along. Not everyone in each group of roving adolescents wanted to go on the same ride. There was a lot of peer pressure to deal with. Some of the students learned that it's perfectly fine, and even fun, to be the guardian of the bags while the others go on a looping coaster. Others learned that there's a fine line between encouraging and bullying—encouraging another to go on a ride feels good, while bullying someone into doing it leaves regret and remorse.

In addition to all of this, the students learned how to manage money. They had to read a map and use technology to discover a schedule. The students learned to take care of their own hygiene and deal with blisters. Most importantly, they learned patience and the art of occupying themselves while in a long line.

Above all, they learned that any hardship was worth it to be able to have fun. Fun makes life worth living; it's why we go to work and why we want to take care of our problems. Too often, children receive only negative messages about work from adults. We need children to learn that work is what gives us the means to have fun and enjoy life.

Theme parks excel at providing fun. They also excel at attaching price tags to the fun. Giving kids a finite amount of money and setting them loose in a theme park is a lesson in priorities, choices, and real consequences. But as real as going hungry at Six Flags might be, it's not nearly as bad as going hungry for months when you're twenty-five because all your money is going into a car you can't afford. Children need to rehearse how to be grown up. Theme parks offer a safe place for that to happen.

Dreamlly's Theme Park Recommendation

Valleyfair
Shakopee, Minnesota

Okay, I'm quite biased when writing about Valleyfair because it is my home park. All theme park enthusiasts have a soft spot for their first park. Please read this disclaimer: Do not plan an entire vacation around Valleyfair. Valleyfair is not a destination park. (Any family that plans a week-long journey to Valleyfair would probably want me to reimburse them for their airfare.) However, if you find yourself in the Minneapolis area during a glorious Minnesota summer, then Valleyfair will provide a complete day of entertainment.

To be fair to the park, Valleyfair is the most northerly located major theme park in North America. At forty-five degrees latitude, it's two degrees farther north than Canada's Wonderland in Toronto. In addition, it's the farthest major park in the world from an ocean. (While Tivoli Gardens in Copenhagen has a more northern latitude, its proximity to the North and Baltic Seas provides weather modulation.) All this means that the climate of Valleyfair includes long winters that can be a bit harsh. In fact, a major blizzard on April 14, 2018, caused Valleyfair to delay its pass holder opening day into mid-May.

Theme parks are businesses that have a bottom line. Attendance dictates that bottom line. And in Minnesota, the calendar dictates the attendance. There will never be a lot of money flowing into a park with as short an operating season as Valleyfair. But with that said, there is still a lot to do here.

Valleyfair holds eight coasters, including the two-hundred-foot Wild Thing. Their award-winning wooden coaster, Renegade, was the first to include a high-speed station fly-by. Valleyfair has a 250-foot drop tower and a 230-foot extreme swing. High Roller is a vintage wooden coaster that shakes and rattles during the entire ride. For theme park history buffs, and for the awkward sixth grader inside of me, High Roller is hard to ignore.

There are plenty of less-extreme rides on the property. Thunder Canyon, a river raft ride, winds its way through a forest of old Minnesota trees. The true star of the park is its nearly one-hundred-year-old carousel. This carousel was built by the famous Philadelphia Toboggan Company. It's one of the last carousels in the world where the entire roof of its building rotates with the horses. It's a real treasure and joy to ride.

Valleyfair includes a water park, Soak City, that does not require separate admission. That's right—for the cost of regular Valleyfair admission, families can enjoy the many slides, wave pool, and lazy river. Just note that, due to the climate, Soak City has a shorter operating season.

When the temperatures get cooler, Valleyfair turns into ValleyScare. It's quite well done, with several scare zones and many complete haunted houses. ValleyScare is definitely not for the easily frightened. I consider it to be fairly intense. This is not a child-friendly environment when it gets dark.

The *valley* in Valleyfair comes from its location right in the middle of the Minnesota River valley. It's twenty miles southeast of the Minneapolis-St. Paul International Airport and the Mall of America. There are a few hotels near Valleyfair, but I'd suggest that a hotel in downtown Minneapolis or closer to the Mall of America will provide more entertainment when the park is closed.

And one last word about the weather. Yes, the famous Minnesota winters are long. However, let this world traveler and lifelong Minnesotan tell you that summer, in this part of the country, is spectacular. I've often said that a summer day in Minnesota is better than any day in Hawaii. The temperatures and humidity are rarely high. In addition, Minnesota has water all over the place. Seriously, you can't turn around without bumping into a lake.

Reason #4:

International theme parks force visitors to interact with locals.

I used to have these adorable nephews. They were small and cuddly. They made me Christmas ornaments that said things like "World's Greatest Uncle." They were always so excited to see me. Then they grew up and started to smell bad. They'd come out of their rooms after hours of playing video games and say things like, "Oh, hey, you're here."

I don't have a problem with video games, and I even believe there are some real skills that can be gained by playing them. However, I do have a problem with the sheer amount of time that my nephews were devoting to their gaming systems. If they'd spent that much time practicing the piano, I'd still be concerned—nobody should fill their entire free time with one activity.

The good news is that I have a magic cure-all for teenageitis: travel. I was confident that traveling outside the United States would teach them new perspectives. But this would not be a quaint visit to a London pub or a weekend on a Costa Rican beach. I wanted them to see the worst of humanity; I wanted them to hear the stories of heartbreak, suffering, and death. They were fifteen and seventeen years old when I convinced their parents to let me take them to Germany.

We had an amazing week, and my goals were accomplished. We toured Munich with a historian and learned about the rise of Nazism. We visited an air raid shelter and read about starvation and complete despair. Most importantly, we spent a day at the Dachau concentration camp hearing the terrible stories of what occurred there. Nobody could visit these places and return home unchanged. But after all that heartbreak, it was time to have some fun. In other words, because they learned how to appreciate their lives it was time to give their lives something to appreciate.

The nephews love roller coasters, and I knew that across Germany lay a theme park with some of the most advanced rides in the world. We rented a car and drove across the country to the French border along the Rhine River. Our destination was Europa-Park—a huge theme park that ranks among the best on the planet.

I would never have let them run around Munich by themselves, but I had no problem with them exploring Europa-Park on their own. They checked in with me from time to time and managed to find their way back to the hotel each night. They told me all about their experiences. But surprisingly, it wasn't the rides that they talked about—it was the atmosphere.

Until I discussed it with them, I'd never realized just how few tourists from North America visit places like Europa-Park. While we were in Munich, we encountered fellow Americans every single place that we visited. (At the Dachau concentration camp, we saw a family of five from Wisconsin that were wearing their full Packers cheese-head garb. It was a Sunday, and the Packers were playing, but still, please, have some respect.) But at Europa-Park, none of us saw or heard another American the entire time we were there.

There were a few times we heard English—very few—and each of these English speakers were British or Irish. Everyone else in lines for the rides spoke German, French, Spanish, Dutch, Italian, or one of dozens of languages spoken across Europe. As teenagers do, my nephews briefly befriended other teenagers while waiting in line. It just happened that in this theme park, all these other teenagers lived somewhere in Europe.

I recently learned that 99.7% of the visitors to Tokyo Disneyland are Japanese. That means only .3% of the park's guests are tourists. You should visit a shine or two if you're ever in Japan, but you'll see more tourists than locals there. If you want to see locals and be surrounded by the Japanese language, you should head to Tokyo Disneyland.

It makes sense when you think about it. DreamWorld, a theme park in Australia, is full of Australians. Most of the visitors to Shanghai Disneyland are from cities in China that I've never heard of. Canada's Wonderland, near Toronto, is packed with Canadians.

Chatting with locals while waiting in line wasn't the only interaction my nephews had at Europa-Park. They had to pay attention to and interpret safety rules that were presented in German. Often, other guests would assist my nephews with seat belts and harnesses. Without me, they were responsible for locating restrooms, ordering food in another language, and navigating the park—all while keeping track of their time and money.

All right, I'll admit it—the motivation for bringing my nephews to Europe wasn't entirely altruistic. I was attempting to win another "world's greatest uncle" prize. But regardless of motive, devoting precious travel resources to a few days at Europa-Park proved to be worth every cent I spent.

Dreamlly's Theme Park Recommendation

Europa-Park
Rust, Germany

Along the gorgeous Rhine River and on the edge of the Black Forest lies Germany's premier theme park. Europa-Park is sixty miles north of Basel, Switzerland, and thirty-five miles south of Strasbourg, France. While the park is entirely in Germany, France is easily seen just on the other side of the river. Rust, Germany, is reachable by train or car. And despite its lack of brand recognition, Europa-Park is a world-class theme park resort and multi-day destination. Just under six million people visited Europa-Park in 2016.

The best part of Europa-Park is its theming. Each land of the park represents a different country with the appropriate architecture, music, and food. I know what some of you are thinking: "Why should I visit a fake Franceland in Germany when real France is right over there?" Well, you shouldn't only visit Europa-Park's Franceland; you should visit both because they are entirely different experiences. The countries represented at Europa-Park include Austria, England, France, Germany, Greece, Iceland, Ireland, Italy, Luxembourg, Netherlands, Portugal, Russia, Scandinavia, Spain, and Switzerland. In addition to these lands, there is the uber-charming Grimm's Enchanted Forest, full of storytelling splendor, and a land based upon a popular European film franchise called *Arthur, In the Minimoys Kingdom*.

Europa-Park is owned and operated by the Mack family. This family is a big deal in the world of theme parks. Believe it or not, the Macks started making themed wagons for circuses in 1780 and have not stopped! Their company, Mack Rides, now builds mega-coasters and other themed rides for theme parks all over the globe. Many of the roller coasters at Knott's Berry Farm, Universal Studios, and even Walt Disney World were born at Mack Rides. It should come as no surprise that their own theme park holds many of the company's best designs. And the designs are pretty darn good, since the Macks have had 240 years to work on them.

Thirteen coasters make their home at Europa-Park, including some of the tallest and fastest in Europe. But of all these high-thrill Mack family inventions, the coaster that keeps me coming back is the rather tame ARTHUR. I don't know anything about the movies that this ride is based on—most Americans don't—but ARTHUR is part coaster and part themed experience. It's amazing.

But there's a lot more than the coasters. In Englandland, there is a train that leaves from a recreated Paddington Station. There are also rides based on London's iconic buses and taxis. Icelandland (I know I'm making up these words, but that's how I roll) has a northern lights whale adventure that is part water ride and part interactive journey. Europa-Park's adorable kids' area is Irelandland. It's full of rides and contains an area to meet the mascot of Europa-Park, Ed EuroMaus.

There is a Leonard da Vinci ride in Italyland and a monorail in Luxembourgland. Swizterlandland includes a Matterhorn-themed coaster and a bobsled ride. Yes, there is also a Matterhorn coaster at Disneyland. Europa-Park has imported several ideas from Mickey, including a geodesic sphere and a pirate ride called Pirates of Batavia. But to be fair, Disney imported a lot of ideas from Europe over the years, so let's just call it even.

I'm not sure how many restaurants are inside the park—there's a lot. My favorite is Foodloop, a restaurant where all the food and beverages are served via roller coaster. It's true! Guests order from screens placed at each table, and trays with the appropriate items come racing down drops and around curves to find the correct table. I've ordered soup, and not one drop was spilled. Foodloop is also a surprisingly cheap place to eat.

There are five beautiful full-service hotels located on the property. I'm partial to Hotel Castillo Alcazar with its medieval castle theme. Several smaller hotels can be found in the village of Rust. Europa-Park is physically connected to Rust; any hotel in the town is walkable from the park. There are many places to camp adjacent to Europa-Park.

The whole property is just so well done, with lots of friendly employees. It's located in a beautiful part of the world that is full of history. Go ahead and explore all the beauty that the Rhine River has to offer. Then spend a few fun-filled days relaxing at Europa-Park and hanging out with Europeans.

Reason #5:

Theme park photographs become part of family collections.

A newsflash for anyone born after 1996: Those of us who grew up prior to the digital age took hardly any photographs because they were expensive and a lot of work. When I went to Valleyfair in the mid-1980s on a sixth-grade band trip, I had a Kodak disc camera. For those unfamiliar with this marvel of human engineering, a Kodak disc camera was this square, flat thing that didn't accept regular thirty-five millimeter film. Instead, you had to go to ShopKo and pay seven thousand dollars for a round disc that, when inserted into the camera, held fifteen photos. That's it—that's all you got for seven thousand dollars.

Consequently, you had to be really, really careful when you took a picture. Because your parents only ever bought you one disc every three years, you could not waste one of your precious fifteen memories on something not worth remembering. When the disc was complete, you took it out of the camera for processing. My town of Sartell, Minnesota, did not have a fancy one-hour photo processing place like they did in the nearby metropolis of

St. Cloud. We had to take our discs to the grocery store and wait four days for them to return.

I believe it cost another seven thousand dollars to pay for the processing. There is, strangely, one thing I really miss about those days: the anticipation of waiting for the photographs was awesome. But we were often—I mean, always—disappointed. It was a mathematical certainty that twelve of the fifteen photos were complete crap.

What was I thinking? I wasted a photo on the Valleyfair sign and still managed to cut off the V and the R. And I thought I looked way cooler than I did in the one picture where some other sixth-grader actually accomplished the difficult task of photographing entire bodies complete with heads. On top of all this was the fact that the Kodak disc camera took terrible pictures that looked oddly pixelated in a time before pixels were even a thing.

After years of repeating this process, we had amassed hundreds of ShopKo photo albums full of the pictures that hadn't ended up in the trash. (Note to millennials: A photo album was a spiral-bound book of empty cardboard adhesive pages that were covered with a plastic film. They were a real pain in the Kodak to use.)

Today, when I look through those old albums, two categories of photographs emerge. There are photos of family members with various types of cakes, and there are photos of family members at theme parks. Why are theme parks so photo-worthy? It's simple—it's because they're fun.

We don't want to remember the times we were bored or had too much homework. Nobody wasted one of their fifteen possible photos on a pile of laundry or on a car stuck in traffic. Theme park photographs are important because we want to relive those times that we felt alive.

In 2017, the most Instagrammed place in the world was Disneyland Resort in Anaheim, California. After Times Square, Central Park, and the Eiffel Tower, Walt Disney World Resort in Florida was the fifth most Instagrammed location in all the realm. Other theme parks to crack the top twenty of Instagrammed places include Universal Studios Hollywood, Santa Monica Pier, Universal Studios Orlando, Tokyo Disney Resort, and Disneyland Paris. In fact, theme parks are the only sites on the list that cost money to view.

The great American photographer and educator Aaron Siskind said, "Photography is a way of feeling, of touching, of loving. What you have captured on film is captured forever ... it remembers little things, long after you've forgotten everything."

We take pictures of the moments we want to remember— that's why you have your camera with you at a theme park and not in line at the dry cleaner. Theme parks offer moments that we want to remember.

I'd like to end this section with one of my favorite quotes ever. It just happens to be about photography.

> "There are no bad pictures; that's just the way your face looks sometimes."
>
> —Abraham Lincoln (Though often attributed to him, Lincoln probably didn't actually say this. Nonetheless, it's hilarious!)

Dreamlly's Theme Park Recommendation

Busch Gardens
Williamsburg, Virginia

Busch Gardens Williamsburg is considered by many enthusiasts as the most beautiful theme park in the United States. It's won a bunch awards for its landscaping and is all around quite photogenic.

Busch Gardens Williamsburg and its sister park in Tampa, Florida, are company parks. Similar to Hersheypark in Pennsylvania, Busch Gardens started as a place for employees of a particular factory. In this case, it was the Anheuser-Busch brewery and bottling plant. However, as the parks expanded and opened their gates to the public, they were sold away from the beer company. Today, both Busch Gardens parks are part of the SeaWorld family. (Although, they both continue to serve beer. Probably a lot of it.)

Williamsburg, Virginia, is famous for its colonial historic district. Busch Gardens is located just a few miles down the road. The area also includes the Jamestown settlement and the Yorktown battlefield. On my initial visit to the area, I was surprised at how thickly the forest covers the landscape. I was expecting to see a more populated east coast setting.

The theme of Busch Gardens Williamsburg is Europe. This may seem an unlikely theme noting the importance of the region to American history. However, the theme is so well done that it works. This is a lesson for us all: If you're committed to an idea that doesn't really fit, give it 110 percent and people will assume it belongs.

Flowing through the center of the park is the enormous Rhine River. This forty-acre body of water was human-made and includes a steep shoreline. A few pedestrian bridges cross the water and create some amazing views. Guests can also walk down to the river (which is really an offshoot of a lake) and take a tour by boat. The banks around the Rhine River are heavily forested and provide an unforgettable sight in the fall.

This is one theme park where a map is imperative. The park's lands are fairly separated from each other. This design adds a lot to the charm of Busch Gardens Williamsburg. To me, it's not that the park is landscaped that well. Instead, park planners have left lots of the natural terrain intact—crossing that terrain between attractions is what makes Busch Gardens so beautiful.

You'll enter through the land of England. This land includes shops, restaurants, and a large replica of Shakespeare's Globe Theater. Shows are an important part of the experience here. Attached to England is, appropriately, Scotland. Here, you can visit the Clydesdale stables. (Holy crap! These are huge and majestic animals.) Scotland also contains places to see sheep and border collies.

Ireland is next. The main draw here is an Irish dance show called *Celtic Fyre.* There is also a small restaurant that offers loaded potatoes in this country/land. As you continue through Ireland, you'll see a large habitat for wolves. The wolves are gorgeous and are featured in educational shows throughout the day.

Somehow, Ireland is attached to France. France leads to a place called New France. New France looks a lot like Canada. In

New France, guests can embark on a train journey around the entire park. This trip is stunning, especially when the train crosses the Rhine River on a tall trestle. Along with the station in New France, there are also stations in Scotland and Festa Italia.

Italy is split into two sections: Italy and Festa Italia. The Italy section looks Renaissance-esque (if that's a word), and Festa Italia has a more modern look. Lastly, there are the lands of Germany and Oktoberfest.

While many people come to Busch Gardens Williamsburg to see the beauty, many others come for the coasters. This ain't your great-great-great-great-grandmother's colonial fun park. Alpengeist has six inversions. Apollo's Chariot has a 210-foot drop. Griffon is a floorless coaster with a 205-foot drive drop straight down. Tempesto has some the highest inversions on the planet. And Verbolten is a multi-launch family coaster. The park's newest coaster, Invadr, is a hybrid-wooden ride that's smooth and fast. Invadr packs a much larger punch than what it looks like from the outside.

My favorite coaster at Busch Gardens Williamsburg is Loch Ness Monster. This vintage ride opened in 1978 and is just as thrilling today. Loch Ness Monster was the world's first steel coaster that included interlocking loops. (One loop goes through the other.) Currently, Loch Ness Monster is the only operating steel coaster left in the world to have interlocking loops. I recently visited the park with a former classmate and her family. Their three kids, all under ten, could not stop shouting, "Again! Again!" each time we completed the ride. This is a special theme park moment for me and a real testament to the quality of Loch Ness Monster. (In case you need a clue, Loch Ness Monster is in the Scotland section.)

Busch Gardens Williamsburg contains a flume ride, a river

raft ride, a highly themed large flume, and a drop tower. Mäch Tower, a 240-foot speeding dropper, is located in the Oktoberfest section of the park. Here is a cool fact: During the holidays, Mäch Tower doesn't drop. Instead, it takes guests slowly up and slowly back down, all so that they can enjoy the many Christmas lights on display.

Speaking of the holidays, Busch Gardens Williamsburg goes all out to present Christmas Town. It's quite an extravaganza with millions of Christmas lights, lots of special food, and a traditional Christmas market in the Oktoberfest area. In addition, there are many holiday-themed shows all over the park.

Virginia's largest water park, Water Country USA, is owned by Busch Gardens and is located just down the road. Busch Gardens does not operate any hotels in the area, but there are plenty to choose from.

Oh—I almost forgot—there is a water blast game located between Italy and Oktoberfest. There's nothing too unusual about the game—except that all the prizes are cute and cuddly stuffed narwhals! I don't know why anyone would not want to win one of these. Do what I did: Play until you win, because cuddly narwhals are priceless. Then take your narwhal and photograph it all over this beautiful park. You will end up with some amazing photos that you will cherish forever.

Reason #6:

Food is spiritual and theme parks offer some of the best on the planet.

One day, Marie Antionette was grooming her little Austrian ponies inside her French Hamlet. She got hungry. What is a queen to do? Even though she wanted to pretend that she was a poor peasant farmer, she wasn't capable of actually cooking anything. So Marie picked up a phone and ordered room service from the palace of Versailles. (By "picked up a phone," I really mean that she sent an actual poor person with a message for the pastry chef.)

Almost immediately, a royal coach arrived at the Hamlet, pulled by four horses. The coach contained hundreds of pastries, puddings, cakes, and enough carbs to make Dr. Atkins completely catatonic. This was the first theme park food, and it certainly wasn't the last. Today, there are literally billions of calories consumed at theme parks every day. I'll start with the fancy stuff and then work down to the tasty snacks that I crave.

Some of the best restaurants in the world are connected to theme parks—most at either a Disney or Universal property. Celebrity chefs abound at Disney Springs and Universal's City

Walk in Orlando. I'm not really into this scene, and it's shocking to see how much money people will spend on food; however, I'm all about enjoying life within your budget—so *bon appetit!*

Many die-hard theme park enthusiasts will say that the best theme park restaurant on the planet is Magellan's at Tokyo DisneySea. It's an incredible Italian Renaissance-themed establishment located inside an enormous recreated fortress. The environment is absolutely stunning, and the service is second to none. I completely understand why people love this restaurant. However, I am not a foodie by any means. I left Magellan's starving after paying seventy US dollars for a tiny chicken bone with a teaspoon of sauce.

You won't find me inside any of the marquee restaurants at Walt Disney World. But that doesn't mean you shouldn't go to them—it also doesn't mean that I go hungry in theme parks. Quite the contrary!

One of my favorite parks is Dolly Parton's Dollywood in Tennessee. I've been there many, many times over the years—however, my best friend, who happens to be from Alabama, had never journeyed inside Dolly's butterfly gates. Last year, I forced her to go with me. As she ate her way through the park, she exclaimed, "This place does southern cooking better than any place in the entire South!"

It's true: If you want to experience the best of Southern cuisine, you must head to Dollywood. It will only set you back seven dollars to grab an entire loaf of Dollywood's signature cinnamon bread. The bread is made from flour that is ground right in front of you. Or you can head to Miss Lillian's Chicken House for the best fried chicken you're likely to have all summer. Or there is Aunt Granny's Buffet with southern sides galore. Or just head on over to … I have to end this paragraph before I pass out just thinking about Dollywood's amazing food.

The best Chinese food I've ever had was in Japan at Vulcania, inside Tokyo DisneySea. It's cheap, delicious, and themed like the inside of a volcano. DisneySea also has Zambini Brothers with better spaghetti Bolognese than you're likely to find in Italy (the real one, not the land at Busch Gardens Williamsburg). I challenge anyone to find a more delicious French crepe than those made fresh at Germany's Europa-Park. The Danes love pølse, a type of hot dog, and they taste better while strolling around Tivoli Gardens' nightly fairy lights.

Even though I want you to learn that theme park food is more than just snacks, it's important not to ignore them—on some days, snacks are the only reason I get out of bed. (Who am I kidding? On all days, snacks are the only reason I get out of bed.) Can anyone resist a Mickey-shaped rice cereal treat dipped in chocolate and covered with sprinkles? Not me. Of course, there are still millions of funnel cakes served at theme parks around the globe, but they come with a lot more topping choices than we ever had when I was a kid.

The Wizarding World of Harry Potter, inside Universal's Islands of Adventure in Orlando, offers cauldron cakes. I won't describe them because it's better for you to discover their greatness all on your own. Ice cream is everywhere, but it's just so much better on a hot day at Australia's DreamWorld. The boysenberry punch at Knott's Berry Farm in California is made from a secret recipe—as it has been for decades. People have written entire books about Epcot's famous Wine and Food Festival in Florida.

Mrs. Claus' Bakery at Holiday World in Indiana smells like my version of heaven. The cookies there taste so much better because you know they were made by Mrs. Claus. Perhaps that's why theme park food tastes special—through food we can intimately experience the fantasy realness of a themed environment. Now, I realize that Dolly Parton isn't personally making all the loaves of cinnamon bread. But I know that she had a part to play in making it possible for me to enjoy it. That's special to me.

Dreamlly's Theme Park Recommendation

Hersheypark
Hershey, Pennsylvania

Here is one park where food isn't just offered—it's the reason the park exists in the first place. The entire past, present, and future of Hersheypark rests with one wonderful food: chocolate. Milton Hershey and his wife did not have any children. Instead, they donated all their money to Hershey, Pennsylvania, a town they founded and built near Mr. Hershey's famous chocolate factory. Hershey is ninety-five miles west of Philadelphia in the middle of Pennsylvania's lush farmland. In fact, Hershey is the only major chocolate brand left on the planet that uses real milk in its process, instead of the powdered version.

There are lots of attractions in Hershey that bear this famous name. It can be a bit confusing. Hersheypark is a sprawling theme park with rides, shows, and attractions—it requires an admission ticket to enter. Chocolate World is a simulated factory tour and ginormous gift shop—it's free to enter. The Hershey Story is a museum that tells the story of Milton Hershey and the history of chocolate—there is an admission charge to enter. In addition to this is the luxurious Hotel Hershey with the expansive Hershey Gardens, twenty-three acres of meticulously groomed beauty.

Hersheypark, the theme park among all this, began as a company park. Milton Hershey opened the park in 1906 as a place for employees and their families to relax. The first roller coaster was added in 1923. In 1971, the park was redeveloped into a commercial theme park under the name Hersheypark. It continues to be owned by the Hershey Company to this day.

Everything is chocolate themed at Hersheypark. I love watching the character show where mascots dressed as iconic Hershey candies come out to dance. They make grand entrances: Hershey's Kiss, Reese's Peanut Butter Cup, Mr. Twizzler, and others. But I'm always surprised to hear the enormous eruption of applause for the most famous character: Plain Milk Chocolate Bar! Yes, regular old Hershey Bar is the Mickey Mouse of Hersheypark.

I've heard there are people out there that eat foods other than chocolate. I really have no concept of that. But if you are one of those that likes to eat from other food groups, then you will have no problem at Hersheypark. There are a lot of offerings here, from sit-down dining to quick-service snacks. Hersheypark even offers salads. (Oh—the horror!)

My favorite food in the park are the Create-Your-Own-Whoopie-Pies. A whoopie pie is a central Pennsylvania staple made of two cake-like cookies sandwiching a layer of thick icing. At Hersheypark, you can choose your own cake and filling flavors. They are delicious!

Oh, yes, there are rides at Hersheypark if you stop stuffing your face long enough to get on one. Thirteen roller coasters make their home in this chocolate paradise, as well as three extreme drop towers. Hershey's Kisses grace the top of the least threatening of the towers, Reese's Peanut Butter Cups adorn the middle tower, and the most extreme tower is dedicated to—you guessed it—plain old Hershey Bar.

My favorite ride at Hersheypark is the monorail. There is no other theme park monorail like it—and I'm including the famous Disney versions. At Hersheypark, the monorail leaves the park's boundaries and travels through a residential area. (I guess when you own the whole town, you can do that sort of thing.) The monorail provides a quick tour of downtown Hershey, complete with its famous Hershey Kiss lampposts, and then runs right over the entrance to the iconic chocolate factory. Do not miss the monorail at Hersheypark.

In addition to all the other rides, over seventy in all, Hersheypark includes a water park called the Boardwalk. It's included in the price of admission. There are several slides, a wave pool, a lazy river, a raft ride, and a hydro-magnetic water coaster.

And if all this wasn't enough, there is a zoo. Milton Hershey discovered that donating schools, hospitals, medical colleges, homes for disadvantaged youth, and gardens was not enough. He also built a zoo. ZooAmerica is connected to Hersheypark and is included with the price of admission. ZooAmerica showcases animals found in North America. Guests can travel between Hersheypark, the Boardwalk, and ZooAmerica as much as they want with one ticket.

Don't forget to stop and visit the statue of Milton Hershey in the middle of the park. This man is a true hero. Not only did he spend his life making other people happy, but he has spent his death doing the same. Hersheypark is an inspiration to the taste buds and to the soul.

Reason #7:

Theme parks have more history.

When we last left the subject of theme park history, Marie Antionette had just opened her little Austrian poor people-themed Hamlet. But less than a decade later, the people of France grew tired of paying for all the extravagance of Versailles—they were also starving. And so, Marie Antionette had to leave her beloved theme park. (She wouldn't have been tall enough to go on any of the rides anyway, now that she was missing a head and all.)

Time moved on, and all over Europe, the crowned heads were replaced with regular heads. But what to do with all the land that formerly belonged to royalty? Much of this land was now designated for public use and became elaborate parks. The grounds of Versailles soon welcomed visitors from all walks of life. Across the continent, the Hapsburg Dynasty decided that opening up their private hunting grounds might appease a restless population—Emperor Joseph II gave this land to the people during the late 1700s. The Prater, Vienna's famous public amusement park, developed during the next two centuries and is still in operation today.

The Prater was a permanent space containing attractions, cafés, and gardens. But it wasn't themed. The next big happening in themed entertainment occurred in 1843. That year, a Danish man named Georg Carstensen convinced his king, Christian VIII, to give him a plot of land near Copenhagen for the purpose of establishing a recreation business. Georg told the king that people weren't able to be concerned about politics if they were busy having fun. He designed and planned his park with unprecedented detail—he named it Tivoli and Vauxhall Gardens, after a garden in Paris and a garden in London, respectively.

Carstensen constructed his buildings to evoke the style of the Orient. Or, more appropriately, the style of what nineteenth-century Danish people thought was the style of the Orient. From the very first day, Tivoli Gardens included cafés, concert stages, gardens, and early forms of mechanical rides. He even constructed a lake in the center of the park and, fitting with the Orient theme, presented fireworks on select nights. There was no admission charged to enter the park, but Carstensen made his money from selling food, drinks, and tickets for the mechanical rides.

What were these mechanical rides like? Were they safe? Well, these rides were the type of contraptions you could probably build in your own backyard—think of a swing set and you'll have a good idea of what people were paying admission to ride. Safety wasn't all that much of a concern because, like I said, there wasn't anything at Tivoli Gardens that was as dangerous as a simple teeter-totter. (Now that I think about it, teeter-totters can be terrifying if the wrong combination of people ride them.)

All that changed in 1889, when Paris hosted the Exposition Universelle, the first epic world's fair of the modern era. Thus began a connection between world's fairs and theme parks that lasted until the 1964-65 fair in New York City. For the 1889 exposition, Paris built an enormous tower that had been designed by a man named Eiffel. You may have heard of this tower or even seen a photograph of it. This tower became a worldwide sensation and, for the first time, a single attraction grew more popular than the fair that created it. People flocked to Paris to ride the elevator to the top of Eiffel's tower. Sure, they also visited parts of the Exposition Universelle, but a ride up the tower provided a thrill and inspired the imagination.

Not to be outdone, the planners of the famous 1893 World's Fair in Chicago solicited ideas from entrepreneurs to create another worldwide sensation. The winning contraption, an enormous wheel built by a man named Ferris, defined the already impressive exposition. Incidentally, the 1893 Chicago World's Fair placed all of its mechanical amusements in a single area that was located on an existing public park. The park chosen to host the amusements sat midway between four neighborhoods—the name of this park was Midway Plaisance. Today, the term *midway* still defines the area of a fair where all the rides are located.

Now, finally, those of us on this side of the pond got to have some of the action that visitors of the Prater and Tivoli Gardens had been experiencing for decades. However, instead of former royal gardens, early amusement parks in the United States were almost exclusively connected to transportation companies. Every major city in the country was in the midst of the Industrial Revolution. It was vital that these cities be able to move workers quickly from their homes to their jobs. Almost overnight, vast networks of trains, trolleys, and streetcars sprang up in towns small and large.

During the week, transportation systems hummed with commuters. But on the weekends, the trolleys were silent. Savvy business tycoons were eager to find a way to get people to pay for transportation on Saturdays and Sundays. The "end-of-the-line" park was born. These amusement parks were built by the trolley companies at the terminus of their tracks—usually, they were located at a place where the tracks met some body of water. Coney Island in Brooklyn and Cedar Point near Cleveland are examples of "end of the line" parks that have survived. (Technically, Coney Island is a place where several parks were and are located. When most people think about Coney Island, they are really thinking about a place called either Luna Park or Astroland.)

On any given weekend between 1895 and 1940, Americans rode trolleys as far as they could and then stepped into a world of amusement. During this period, the "gravity railroad," a type of elevated train that used gravity to propel its cars, evolved into the modern roller coaster. Cedar Point, an end-of-line park, is now the roller coaster capital of the world. And, yes, it all began with a simple train that had a little hill.

Again, time moved on, and the world found itself at war. The Nazis burned down most of Copenhagen's beloved Tivoli Gardens—it was one of the first places that the Danes restored after the Allied victory. In the United States, the military men and women returned. But this time, they ditched the trollies for cars.

The automobile spelled death for the hundreds of American "end-of-the-line" amusement parks. People no longer rode the trolley and were free to drive for hours. Due to dramatically decreased revenue, amusement parks employed unsavory people, and they fell into disrepair. Families no longer felt comfortable visiting, and most of these parks soon disappeared. As 1950 rolled around, it seemed like amusement parks were a thing of the past.

As the leisure park industry was dying, on the west coast, a woman named Lillian remarked to her husband that amusement parks were horrible places full of crime and dirt. Her husband listened to her and wondered why amusement parks were full of crime. He wondered if there was a way to keep amusement parks clean. He wondered if he could build a park that was different. Lillian's husband was named Walt—stay tuned.

Dreamlly's Theme Park Recommendation

Tivoli Gardens
Copenhagen, Denmark

Tivoli Gardens is just as delightful to visit today as it was when it first opened. Due to centuries of growth, the park is no longer outside Copenhagen, but right smack-dab in the middle of it! For theme park fans, Tivoli Gardens is just as much a Mecca as Disneyland and Cedar Point.

Easily reached via train from anywhere in Copenhagen, Tivoli Gardens offers modern thrill rides combined with its historical Eastern-themed environment. There are several types of admission tickets offered. Visitors can purchase a cheaper ticket that doesn't include rides or an all-day pass that includes every ride on the premises. There are options between those two as well.

Full of restaurants and cafés, Tivoli Gardens is one of Europe's best dining opportunities. Every cuisine imaginable can be found inside its gates. During the afternoon, you will see many Europeans enjoying coffees and teas. At night, Tivoli Gardens becomes one the largest nightclubs in the world. Thousands of people hang out with their favorite beverages. This is not your grandmother's magic kingdom, and I wouldn't recommend Tivoli Gardens for children after 8:00 p.m. But for the rest of us, it's a real hoot.

The most spectacular aspect of Tivoli Gardens are its many landscaped gardens. Centuries-old foliage curves gracefully around ponds and lakes. Whichever time of year you choose to visit, you will see brilliant displays of colors and floral creations. Tivoli Gardens at night is extraordinary, as millions of small white lights illuminate the buildings and grounds. This is one park where you'll want to take your time and stroll.

Side note: I've ridden many roller coasters in my time. But none as terrifying as Tivoli's 1914 coaster. It's so old, in fact, that it doesn't have a name. The roller coaster at Tivoli Gardens is terrifying because (a) it's so freaking old, and (b) it's just so freaking old! An operator actually sits in the middle of the train with his/her hands on a large iron lever. I'm not joking here! The iron lever is the coaster's braking system. The seat safety device is some sort of rope that you tie around yourself and hope that it's strong enough. This would all be fine on some kiddie-coaster, but the roller coaster contains some substantial drops and whips along at an extraordinary pace. There are no computerized brake runs on this century-old track. And as if all this wasn't enough, if the operator isn't strong enough to pull the lever all the way back, you'll have to ride again and again until he or she musters the strength to stop the train. To ride this coaster is to truly say that you have ridden through history.

Reason #8:

Making a pilgrimage is often part of the theme park experience.

Very few people have ever lived inside a theme park. Walt Disney had an apartment above the fire station inside Disneyland's Main Street, USA. Over at Nashville's Opryland, Roy Acuff, country music legend, lived in a house inside the park. He'd often sit on the porch, and if you waved to him, he'd invite you up to sit with him. (This is absolutely true. But don't make the trip today because Acuff died in 1992 and Opryland closed permanently in 1997.) Before the completion of Dollywood's DreamMore Resort, Dolly Parton had an apartment above Apple Jack's Restaurant in the Rivertown Junction section of her park. She had one closet for all her shoes and another closet for all her wigs. (This may or may not be true.) But for the rest of us who don't live in a theme park, we have to make a journey to get to our themed dreamlands.

Like the word *shrine*, *pilgrimage* is another term that reminds people of a religious experience. Again, I mean no disrespect by using the word here because, for me, the journey to my dream escapes is a spiritual pilgrimage. It's a fact of life that most of us have to travel to experience a theme park—they're not as easy to access as, say, the grocery store or McDonald's.

The act of travel requires action. Even if you're just driving ten miles to your local park, you still have to invest some energy into the process. The energy you need is physical, mental, and emotional. There is a certain level of commitment involved in visiting a park—it doesn't matter if it's your first visit or if you have a season pass and can't remember how many times you've been there.

Even die-hard Disney fans complain about it, but I love the physical journey to the Magic Kingdom at Walt Disney World in Florida. If you're not familiar, to access the most-visited theme park on the planet, you must make your way across Seven Seas Lagoon. One does not simply drive up to the Magic Kingdom and walk to the gate. There are a variety of transportation options, including monorail, small boat, ferry boat, and resort bus. Sure, when you're anxious to get inside, the trip can be frustrating. But I love that the physical journey serves to separate me from the real world.

You can't just find yourself at Europa-Park; you have to journey there. Rust, Germany, is a couple of hours from any major city. You must either drive or take a train to arrive at Europa-Park. The physical act of moving yourself across the Black Forest is amazing and prepares you for your upcoming experience. Similarly, nobody just happens upon Ocean Park in Hong Kong. You have to have moved your body, somehow, across the island of Hong Kong from Victoria Harbor. A physical pilgrimage, despite the tired butt, is worth the toil.

During the summer of 2006, I tore my Achilles tendon in a running accident. I had surgery and was in a wheelchair for the entire summer—all three months of prime theme park time! I had prepared myself for the physical limitations of being in a wheelchair, but I was quite surprised at the mental exhaustion I experienced. I couldn't just go to Target to buy some eggs. Before I left home, I had to think about how I would get into the store, how I'd reach the eggs, how I'd pay for them, and how I'd get them back home. In the same way, pilgrimages require mental forethought.

When it comes to theme parks, there are a multitude of issues that must be thought about. What time to get there? What type of ticket should I have? How do I get the ticket? What should I wear? Will the park be crowded? Should I bring some water? Etc. All these small mental decisions require energy.

I've found that I revel in the mental aspect of the pilgrimage. It's a privilege for me to be able to spend time thinking about whether Cedar Point will be crowded or not. Similar to with Christmas, thinking about all these tasks is exhausting, but at the same time, they are an integral part of the experience. We've heard so many times, "It's the thought that counts." This sentiment is true when considering the mental pilgrimage required of travel.

People don't usually think about their emotions in terms of energy, but anyone who's experienced a kid crashing after a morning of fun will know that happiness burns a lot of calories. The emotional pilgrimage required to journey to a theme park halfway around the globe is substantial—but it's no greater than the emotions used to chaperone a bus of sixth-graders just ten miles.

Emotions are tricky things. We crave some of them, despise others, and flat-out don't understand the rest. But that's what makes us alive. Theme parks trigger an emotional pilgrimage that I've learned to love.

Someday, you might own a theme park. What a day that would be! You could just wake up, put on your wig, and stumble down some steps. Until then, learn to embrace the pilgrimage.

Dreamlly's Theme Park Recommendation

Shanghai Disneyland
Shanghai, China

Guests have to make a decisive pilgrimage in order to visit Shanghai Disneyland. If you've just accidentally found yourself at a Chinese theme park, then I'd like to meet you—you must have one heck of a story.

To visit China, most travelers from the United States and Europe will need a visa. Obtaining a Chinese visa can be time-consuming and expensive. It will require two visits by you, or your agent, to a Chinese consulate located in your home country. The regulations change often, so it's best to research the process prior to beginning the visa hunt. Find out where the nearest Chinese consulate is located and connect with them directly online for information.

China offers a 144-hour visa-free option for visitors from many countries, including the United States and the European Union. However, there are many restrictions and specifications that must be followed in order to be eligible. The rules change frequently and don't allow for you to return directly to your home country after leaving China. (It's all quite bizarre. I've tried but have never been able to figure out the rationale for many of the rules.) Again, use the internet to learn about the 144-hour visa-free visit to China.

Hopefully, you've found a way to legally enter the People's Republic of China, and you are free to visit the fantastic Shanghai Disneyland. Donald Duck's newest home opened in Shanghai in June of 2016. It's the first international theme park inside mainland China. (We'll talk later about Hong Kong, which is also in China, and why it's a bit of a special situation.) The best part of Shanghai Disneyland is that everything is brand spanking new with technology that will blow your freaking mind. I don't say this lightly—the park is years ahead of anything we've seen in the US.

For example, let's look at a classic Disney attraction found around the globe: Peter Pan's Flight. Around the globe, the Disney guests board small fiberglass ships and are lifted through the window in the Darlings' London home. The ship soars along the ceiling as the passengers sail high above London and then travel to Neverland via the second star on the right. No matter which Disney Park you're at, it's a nice journey and quite worth the wait.

However, Peter Pan flies differently in Shanghai. Here, the ships have a lot more technology, which allows them much more freedom of movement. They can speed up and slow down to emphasize different parts of the story. They can rise up to the ceiling and crash into a pool of water, turning at will so that the passengers always have the best view. In Shanghai, the ships can turn on a dime to sail up and around Captain Hook's pirate ship. While the ride is lovely at the other parks, it's jaw-dropping and awesome in Shanghai.

The most awesome example of Shanghai's technological difference is their version of Pirates of the Caribbean. You're probably already familiar with the iconic Disney attraction where guests sit in a boat and float though scenes of pirate antics. Yes, it glorifies a lot of bad behavior (please see reason #17 for more about this situation). Basically, the boats float at will, and then everybody leaves at the end of the ride.

At Shanghai Disneyland, the boats for Pirates of the Caribbean aren't really boats at all. They sit in water—just for effect—but they are really ride vehicles that are attached to an intricate ride system. You'll know something is different when you're asked to strap a safety harness around yourself. These "boats" move at various speeds. They can go forward and backward. In one amazing scene, your boat is floating past a large pirate ship, only to be sucked inside the ship as water gushes through a hole.

Even simple attractions have received a high-tech treatment in Shanghai. Walk-though attractions that tell the story of a princess or two can be found at most Disney Parks. They are always cute and well executed. At Disneyland Paris, the story of Sleeping Beauty is told through beautiful stained-glass windows.

The Once Upon a Time Adventure inside the castle at Shanghai Disneyland tells the story of Snow White in a creative technological manner. The vignettes that tell the story are all interactive and respond to what the guests are doing in front of them. I don't want to give too many spoilers here, but feel free to wave your arms around a lot. The best part of the experience is that after a bit, the interactions stop as a signal that you should move on to the next vignette. This is a fantastic way of keeping guests moving throughout the attraction without a few overzealous fans holding up the entire line.

Speaking of the castle, Shanghai Disneyland's Enchanted Storybook Castle is the largest of all the Disney castles. It holds two attractions, one beautiful restaurant, a complete theatrical stage, and several shops. It's truly a functional castle that can be seen for miles around.

The grounds of Shanghai Disneyland are gorgeous. A Disney-made lake, Wishing Star Lake, serves as the centerpiece for the entire property. Wishing Star Park is a public park that connects the theme park to a nearby train station. This public park is managed and maintained by Disney—there is no admission charged to enter.

My favorite spot in all of Shanghai Disneyland is the Garden of the Twelve Friends. This splendid garden contains intricate mosaics representing each of animals in China's New Year's zodiac. The animals are, of course, from Disney films. The year of the dog is represented by Pluto and the year of the rat by Remy from *Ratatouille.* This garden is quite special to me because my animal is represented by a Disney animal from my home state. I was born in the year of the ox (those of you familiar with Chinese culture might be able to figure out my age if you're also good at math). The ox is represented by Babe the Blue Ox from Disney's 1958 short film *Paul Bunyan.* Paul finds Babe stuck in the snow in a northern Minnesota forest. When I visit Babe at Shanghai Disneyland, it makes me feel like I'm home.

Shanghai Disney Resort includes two hotels. The Toy Story Hotel is a cheaper option with lots of fun theming. It's a good experience to eat at this hotel's café, even if you aren't staying there. The more expensive option is the spectacular Disneyland Hotel. It's beautiful with lovely views of Shanghai Disneyland.

In addition to the two hotels, the resort contains DisneyTown. This large shopping and dining area is similar to Downtown Disney in California. There is no admission charged to visit. DisneyTown includes a large Disney store and a fully functional Broadway theater. Currently, a Mandarin version of Disney's *Beauty and the Beast* is playing in the theater for an additional charge.

Should you decide to take a pilgrimage to this part of the world, there is a lot to do both inside and outside Shanghai Disneyland. The amazing city of Shanghai is easily accessible from the theme park. Nothing will feel like home when you're visiting Shanghai, but that's sort of the point of a pilgrimage.

Reason #9:

Memories are formed when the out-of-the-ordinary occurs; theme parks excel at that.

You probably don't remember a trip you took to the grocery store last December 17. But you would remember that trip if your boyfriend proposed to you at the grocery store on that day. Or you might remember it if it were December 25 instead of 17. And you surely remember a trip you took to the grocery store yesterday. This is all because our brains don't have the resources to remember everything. In order for an item to move from short-term to long-term memory, it must be—well—memorable.

Screaming your head off on an inverted roller coaster might be memorable enough to commit to long-term memory. Watching your brother scream his head off on an inverted coaster will certainly make the cut into your permanent brain. You don't see your brother screaming every day. That memory is worth whatever energy you expended to get inside the park.

Theme park memories from my younger years almost always involve the rides themselves. I remember my first ride on the High Roller like it was yesterday. I also remember the first ride on

Wild Rails—a Valleyfair coaster that was long ago sent to coaster heaven. I can remember being terrified of the carousel horses that went up and down. Seriously, my earliest memories involve an intense struggle to find the stationary horses. (I was probably the only kid ever that wanted to sit on the carousel bench that was usually full of grandmas.)

As I got older, my memories grew less about rides and much more about people. I'm sure you have all seen those extremely sappy commercials that Disney airs during the winter. They usually show the perfect family having the most perfect day at a Disney Park. You may think these ads are too good to be true. The thing is, though, Disney commercials are not misleading. It's so easy to form memories inside theme parks because they are just so darn memorable. My own family is far from perfect, yet I have these perfect memories of them at Dollywood.

One of the best stories I've ever seen on television is a two-part episode of ABC's *The Middle* where the Heck family goes to Walt Disney World. The Hecks are not perfect—that's pretty much what *The Middle* is all about. Their visit to the Magic Kingdom begins with the normal pitfalls. The kids are crabby and don't get along. The parents are tired, and lines are long. The middle kid had to go to the first aid building. They try to take that most iconic of all family photos in front of Cinderella Castle. Not even the photo works out.

Anyway, as usually occurs in real life, their vacation starts to turn around as soon as they stop trying so hard. Frankie Heck, the most realistic mom on television, decides to give up on the magic. She sends each kid in his or her own direction and goes off with the dad. It's a horrible thing for a family to split up at the Magic Kingdom, but in many cases, splitting up will be the most wonderful horrible thing that could ever happen. The kids end up sticking together and start to have fun without a plan. (Siblings, even those who bicker constantly, always know that it's more fun to stay together.) Mom and Dad have a nice dinner in Epcot's Franceland. (On television, people can get from park to park at Walt Disney World almost instantly. This does not happen in real life.) Eventually, the Hecks get together just in time for fireworks. While the Heck family isn't perfect, they have a perfectly imperfect day.

I know what you're thinking: "Well, Mickey Mouse owns ABC, and of course, the scripted television family was mandated to have a great time at Walt Disney World." Yes, that's all true—but that doesn't make it any less real. I have had many, many days in theme parks where the very Heck phenomenon happened to my family. I remember total and complete breakdowns that were fixed instantly with a soaking ride on the river rafts. There is some actual magic inside theme parks, and this is it!

After we've arrived back home, we carry the memory of that river raft ride with us. When another complex situation arises— and they always do—we remind ourselves of our theme park moment. If we could all exist together in harmony at Dollywood, then we can find a way to exist together in harmony back in Minnesota.

Theme parks excel at creating a fantasy. But there is nothing made-up about my memories—they are all real. Memories are worth more than money to me. Memories are definitely more useful than perhaps anything you can buy.

Dreamlly's Theme Park Recommendation

Magic Kingdom
Walt Disney World, Florida

Here it is, folks, the most-visited theme park in all the realms. The Magic Kingdom, aka the most magical place on Earth, is one of four theme parks that comprise the Walt Disney World Resort. In this book, I've highlighted just two of the four parks. For more information, including lots of history, get a copy of my book *World Traveler's Guide to Disney,* available on Amazon.com. (Now back to our regularly scheduled writing.)

I think it's safe to say that more children have dreamed about this theme park than any other. It opened in 1971, just when all of us Generation Xers were being born. Of course, Disneyland had been around for sixteen years prior, but one of the key differences between these properties is scope. Disneyland has always been a local park visited by lots of Californians. But from the start, Walt Disney World in Florida was designed and marketed to be a world destination. For better or worse, many Disney fans will put it like this: Disneyland was built by a father for his daughters, while Disney World was built by a committee for a horde of tourists.

There is nothing more memorable than your first glimpse of an iconic Disney castle. For most people in the United States, that castle is the Magic Kingdom's Cinderella Castle. It looks right at home at the end of Main Street, USA. (Just a side note: *Cinderella Castle* is not a typo, and it's not missing the apostrophe S. It's a Disney thing, so it's best just to go with it.)

I'm sure that there are around ten billion guide books devoted to the Magic Kingdom. And most of you are familiar with the classic attractions like Pirates of the Caribbean, Space Mountain, The Haunted Mansion, and "it's a small world." Instead, I'd like to write about things you can do to create memories without waiting in much of a line. (Another side note: "it's a small world" is always written in quotes and without capitalization. It's a Disney thing, so it's best ... you know the drill.)

Walt Disney's Enchanted Tiki Room in Adventureland is rarely full of people. Tropical birds, flowers, and tikis sing inside this air-conditioned pavilion. Similarly, the Country Bear Jamboree is just up the path in Frontierland. Here, you'll be entertained (sort of) by dozens of bears. It's endearing and never at capacity. Head to these attractions if you're looking for instant air-conditioning on a hot Florida day.

Across from the Country Bear Jamboree, take a ride on the riverboat. There's always room for you on a relaxing journey around Tom Sawyer Island. This attraction is not air-conditioned, so opt for it either really early or really late. Right outside the riverboat landing, catch a performance of *The Muppets Present Great Moments in History ... But Only the American Parts.* It's hilarious, with plenty of room to view the show.

In Fantasyland, Mickey's Philharmagic is always available without a line. This 4-D show is spectacular and represents Disney at its finest. If you're interested in something a little more nostalgic, head to Tomorrowland for a performance of the Carousel of Progress. This rotating theater, from the 1964-65 World's Fair in New York, tells the story of a family through the twentieth century. It's very dated, but air-conditioned. It's also long, but air-conditioned. It's somewhat confusing at times and just plain incorrect, but it's air-conditioned.

My favorite attraction in the entire park, and one that rarely has a line, is directly across from the Carousel of Progress. Take a ride around the Tomorrowland Transit Authority Peoplemover. The views are fantastic as you ride in small carts above the crowds. It's relaxing, quiet, and smooth. And as a bonus, while riding the Peoplemover, you will take a journey through the bottom of the air-conditioned Space Mountain.

The Magic Kingdom is famous for its parades and fireworks. Check the times when these events will occur. The nightly fireworks show offers way more than pyrotechnics. There are loads of special effects and unbelievable projections that make the castle appear in various forms. Universal Studios has started to step up its parade game, but for the most part, Disney reigns supreme when it comes to theme park parades. They've got this down.

Just like when it comes to parades, nobody does any sort of holiday better than Disney. Christmas is as storybook as you can get inside the Magic Kingdom. Tasteful decorations are everywhere, along with millions of sparkling lights. Cinderella Castle is literally aglow. There are more poinsettias and wreaths on Main Street, USA, than you have seen in your life. If the regular Disney parades are great, then the Christmas Disney parades are indescribable. On certain nights in November and December, the Magic Kingdom closes early for regular guests and reopens for Mickey's Very Merry Christmas Party. You need a separate ticket for this event, but you'll get a special parade, stage show, fireworks, character greetings, and—all the cookies you can eat— *and*—all the hot chocolate you can drink! It's truly a magical experience.

Next to Christmas, Halloween is starting to run a very close second. However, don't think of Halloween at the Magic Kingdom as a horror-filled scare fest. This is more of a "really cute fall festival with adorable costumes" kind of Halloween. The decorations are just as well done as they are at Christmas. The creativity always astounds me. Just as with Christmas, on certain nights the Magic Kingdom closes to host Mickey's Not-So-Scary Halloween Party. This party comes with a special parade, fireworks, amazing stage show, character greetings, and—all the candy you can eat! The *Hocus Pocus Villain Spectacular,* presented only during these parties, is the best Disney show on Earth.

As for the rest of the "world," there are gazillions of themed hotel resorts both on and off Disney property. Disney-owned hotels will always be more expensive, but they come with perks like special theme park hours for guests. Along with the resorts are the three other theme parks and two water parks. Disney Springs, pretty much a theme park in itself, is a free shopping and dining district located at Walt Disney World. Then, you also have several golf courses, lots of spas, wedding facilities, ESPN's Wide World of Sports, amazing pools, and pretty much anything else your dream destination could ever offer.

Of all the theme parks that I'm highlighting in this book, the Magic Kingdom is the one that requires the most planning. Don't just wake up in Florida and decide to head there on the spur of the moment. You need to do your research on this one. There is a lot of work behind the scenes to create the magic of the Magic Kingdom. You will also need to do some behind-the-scenes work to make a magical and memorable day.

Reason #10:

Human brains can wander and escape harsh realities at theme parks.

I've used the word *escape* several times already and probably will use it several times more. It's an important need that I equate with feeling safe and loved. Let's face it: Life is hard for all of us.

One evening during a cold Minnesota winter, I was late for a meeting, and a tire blew out while I was driving my 2003 Ford Focus down the freeway. I don't know if you've ever had a tire blow out at seventy miles per hour, but it's absolutely terrifying. (Much worse than the carousel horses that go up and down.) The sound of the car was horrific as I managed to get over on the shoulder. Fortunately, I was fine, and there were no other cars near mine at the time.

So there I sat, in the middle of nowhere at five degrees Fahrenheit as I waited for a tow truck. As it often happens, one terrible event triggers a litany of pity that the human brain cannot stop. Out of frustration, I called one of my friends and couldn't stop complaining about how miserable my life was. She replied, "Well, some people went through the Holocaust, so I'm sure you can get through this."

What she said about the Holocaust was true. There were millions of worse situations I could have been in. I then felt bad for feeling bad. Some years later, I told my husband, a psychiatrist, about that night. He said, "Yes, it's true that it's worse to be in a concentration camp than to be stuck on a road. However, it's important to know that being stuck on a cold road is still a problem—it was your problem, and it was completely all right to worry and commiserate."

I told you this story to let you know that it's perfectly fine to need an escape. I doubt that even the Queen of England is comfortable all the time. She needs an escape and has the right to explore one. She may wake up one morning and despise the face of Prince Phillip. Perhaps she takes her mind back to the time that she and Winston Churchill rode the tiny carousel outside the Tesco on Bleeker Street. (Come to think of it, why hasn't the Queen of England opened her own theme park? Think of the revenue she could gain! She'd have awesome food, and the character meet-and-greets would be amazing!)

All kidding aside, there is a core group of ultimate escape memories that are locked in my brain. Some people refer to these memories as their "happy place." When I'm at the dentist and need to go to my happy place, my brain wanders off to Tokyo DisneySea. This park is so amazingly fantastic that it easily seared itself into long-term memory. There's nothing like it in the world—that's why it's so out of the ordinary. I can picture my husband and me walking through the entrance plaza with such clarity that it's like I'm watching a film. I can smell the unique flavors of DisneySea popcorn. By the time I complete a virtual tour of DisneySea in my mind, the dentist is finished.

But it's not just the memories that provide an escape. The actual act of visiting a theme park provides a physical escape that benefits our mental health. You may be able to check your smart phone periodically inside a theme park. But it's impossible to be tied to technology like you are in the real world. Nobody can reach you when you're on an attraction or watching a show. A roller coaster may only last two minutes, but that's two minutes when you are completely aware of yourself and your surroundings.

Some people refer to Walt Disney World Resort as a bubble. They use the term to describe the safety and comfort of a place that strives to be as unreal as possible. Disney World has become an escape for millions of people. But your escape doesn't have to be Disney World—it doesn't even have to be in Florida. You can escape to your nearest theme park and have a day of fun. This day of fun will be an immediate escape from the real world, and this day will provide memories that can be used for unlimited future escapes.

The Sound of Music, while being an amazing movie, does not always provide the best advice. You don't have to "Climb Every Mountain" right now. The concept of escape is not always negative. It's okay to take a break from climbing your mountain to have some fun. Think about this: A *Sound of Music* theme park where you can ride the Climb Every Mountain Roller Coaster— now, that's an escape I'd like to try.

Dreamlly's Theme Park Recommendation

Hong Kong Disneyland
Hong Kong SAR, China

Before you can understand why I chose Hong Kong Disneyland to represent a park that provides an escape from harsh realities, you need to have just a bit of information about the political construction of the area. Due to a very old treaty as a result of the long-ago Opium Wars, Hong Kong was under British rule for almost a century. Britain designed and built the city—the citizens enjoyed all the freedom associated with being a part of the United Kingdom. All that changed on July 1, 1997, when the treaty dictated that Hong Kong be handed back to China. Queen Elizabeth II sent Prince Charles to literally hand over the necessary documents to the leaders of China's communist party.

This time was marked with turmoil for the residents of Hong Kong. Imagine living in a democracy one day and being at the whim of a communist regime the next. Consequently, to stop a stream of Hong Kong residents that were using their British citizenship to emigrate before 1997, certain plans were made to appease the population. Hong Kong became part of China, but also remained fairly Hong Kong-ish.

Hong Kong exists as a Special Administrative Region (SAR) within the People's Republic of China. The region kept its own money, the Hong Kong dollar, along with its own border policies.

Citizens of the United States and European Union do not need a visa to visit Hong Kong. The people of Hong Kong kept a local system of governance, and they were not subject to China's "one child per family" policy.

However, in recent years, things have started to change a bit. The central communist party in Beijing has a desire to take more control over Hong Kong. In 2016, information became available that Beijing had fixed the results of Hong Kong's most recent election. Massive demonstrations broke out upon the streets of Hong Kong. There has been continuing resistance against Beijing since that time.

The normal tourist in Hong Kong will probably not notice any of this. But the people of Hong Kong realize all the subtle ways that things are changing. The Hong Kong press isn't as free as it once was, and other regulations sort of sneak their way into existence. Consequently, there has been some violence propagated against mainland Chinese visitors to Hong Kong. On a scale of 1 to 10, where 10 is an all-out war and 1 is a basket of puppies, I'd say the current tension level is about 3.8—nothing that should stop travelers from visiting, but enough tension to impact the attitudes of people living in the area.

Okay, enough of all this political crap; let's talk about Disneyland. (That sigh of relief you just exhaled is the escape that I'm talking about.) Hong Kong Disneyland opened on a beautiful bay and day in 2005. It's located on an island right outside Hong Kong proper, Lantau Island, which is also the home of Hong Kong International Airport. Of all the Disney Parks on the planet, Hong Kong Disneyland has the most spectacular natural location, with lush mountains and lovely views of the ocean.

Hong Kong Disneyland is small, and that's part of its charm. The resort is comprised of Hong Kong Disneyland and three beautiful hotels. There are no loud shopping districts or water parks. There are also no crowds. Hong Kong Disneyland is the least attended of the Disney Parks, which makes it a relaxing and charming place to visit.

Inside the park you will find the classic lands and attractions that are loved around the world. Hong Kong Disneyland has the world's best version of the famous Jungle Cruise. This edition of the iconic attraction meanders through a real jungle and includes sights not seen in the other Disney Parks. Riders on this attraction wait in a queue determined by which languages they'd like to hear on the voyage: English, Mandarin, or Cantonese. (Hong Kong has two official languages, for now: English and Mandarin.)

When the park opened, it was rather tiny, with just four classic lands: Main Street, USA, Adventureland, Fantasyland, and Tomorrowland. Since that time, new mini-lands have been added along the perimeter of the park. These mini-lands set Hong Kong Disneyland apart from the others. Mini-lands allow the Imagineers the time and resources to plan every square inch of a small area. Hong Kong Disneyland is immensely intricate and immersive.

Grizzly Gulch is a mini-land themed after the American west. Here, you can ride Big Grizzly Mountain Runaway Mine Cars, a family coaster that goes both forward and backward. Another mini-land, Mystic Point, includes the amazing Mystic Manor. This is Hong Kong Disneyland's version of the Haunted Mansion. Many theme park enthusiasts consider Mystic Manor to be the best ride-through dark ride in existence.

Toy Storyland is a third mini-land that includes attractions based on the *Toy Story* franchise. A mini-land attached to Tomorrowland is themed after the Marvel comic characters, including a major Iron Man attraction. An Ant Man experience is currently under construction.

I need to give you a warning about the weather. Hong Kong is one of those cities that we don't think about in terms of weather. But this city is located within the tropics. It's hot and very, very humid. Think of it like Florida on steroids—lots of steroids. In fact, it's so much worse than Florida that I won't visit Hong Kong between April and November.

While visiting Hong Kong Disneyland, take time to appreciate the natural beauty of its environment. You will feel far removed from the nearby cosmopolitan city of Hong Kong. Lantau Island is literally a tropical island with rolling mountains of lush, green vegetation. Even though the theme park is quite close to Hong Kong International Airport, you won't see any of it from the resort itself.

For a stunning view, follow the manicured garden path that connects Hong Kong Disneyland with the Disneyland Hotel. This path will lead directly to a ferry dock on the South China Sea. Stand at the edge of the dock and look out over the water. You'll be able to see the amazing skyline of Hong Kong in the distance. Spend a few moments thinking about how fortunate you are to be able to escape in this cozy resort.

Reason #11:

Each person walks about this planet with a small child inside; theme parks let that kid out.

It boggles my mind how hard adults work every day to be seen by others as adults. I once worked with a woman who always walked around with a large stack of binders. I often wondered how she managed to carry the stack without dropping any of them. She frequently darted from here to there and was the champion of calling meetings to discuss what we should discuss at the next meeting. She made it a point that everybody knew she was at work before anyone else and she stayed until the last car had left the parking lot.

I tried hard to avoid her—her philosophy of living was just not healthy for me to experience. However, one Friday, I was stuck with her and her binders in an elevator.

"What are your plans for the weekend?" I asked. (It's the standard question to ask in elevators on Fridays.)

"I'll be here," she replied, "I have so much work to do. I really envy you, Michael. You get to take so many vacation days."

I couldn't believe that she'd said that. In my world, those were fighting words.

"Yes," I answered, "I never leave a vacation day unused—that's quite true. I believe that spending time with my husband is more important than any project I could ever have here. I also love to spend time with myself."

"Well, I wish I could say that. But the fact is that my projects really are way too important."

What I wanted to say: "No, your projects are not important at all. You're just telling yourself that to justify your lousy existence. Work is your way of avoiding your family and yourself. If your work was really that important, you'd have finished it by now."

What I did say: "My projects are also impor … never mind. You have a good weekend, anyway."

Here is the best part of the story. A few months later, we were both early for a meeting. She left me alone in a conference room with her binders when she went to the restroom. (I guess she was human after all!) So there I sat—all by myself with those precious binders. I'm not shy when it comes to people who diss my vacations. I quickly got up and looked through the binders because I was curious. You won't believe this—the binders contained empty pages! All of them, except for the top one, were filled with plain old copy paper. She'd spent years carrying around fake binders so that people would believe she was busy. I was sad for her, but only for a moment. It was her own fault.

This former coworker desperately needed to go to a theme park. Somewhere, deep inside, was a little girl who was literally dying to have some fun. It probably would not have made a difference for me to explain my philosophy to her. If I'd told her about her inner child, she would have just come up with another excuse to stop truly living. Why? Because humans are intrinsically lazy, and it's just so easy to fit in. For her to have fun would mean she'd have to face her family. She'd also have to acknowledge that she wasn't all that special when it came to work. These are difficult tasks, indeed. It's easier to play the part of the world's best worker.

My favorite part of the Christian Bible is from the Gospel of Mark. In this section, Jesus tells the people that the only way to enter heaven is by approaching it through the wonder and awe of a child. I don't take these words lightly and have little regard for those who disagree with me.

I actually pity people who don't get excited for Halloween. For me, the saddest day of the entire year is December 26, because it means that Christmas is a whole year away. I still love my birthday, and cartoons, and stuffed animals. When I'm depressed and feeling down, my husband knows that the best thing he can do is get me a set of Legos. After a couple of hours building with Legos, I'm refreshed. (Remember, my husband is a psychiatrist, so Legos are almost a medical necessity.)

Theme parks are specifically constructed to make you feel like a child. What is a roller coaster if not a manifestation of a dad playing "airplane" with his kids? On a carousel, you get to safely ride an animal around in a circle. It's more than the imagined fun of riding a colorful animal. It's also reminding us of what it was like to be in the womb. (Yep, I went there—and I'm not ashamed of it.)

Theme parks offer a world full of the emotions that we almost exclusively reserve for children: wonder, excitement, glee, anticipation, and most of all, fun. I'm calling to all of you: Put down your fake binders. Take all your vacation days. Experience life through the eyes of a child. Let those inner kids out, no matter how freaky they are. Set those kids free and let them have fun.

Legoland
Winter Haven, Florida

Anyone who doesn't like playing with Legos is evil and probably shouldn't be trusted. If you haven't built anything with Legos in a while, you should go and get some. It doesn't matter how old you are. Just a few minutes connecting and disconnecting a simple of row of Legos is therapeutic and good for the soul.

There are several Legolands around the globe. The American locations include Florida and California. A new Legoland will open near New York City in 2020. I'd like to focus on Legoland Florida because of its unique attractions and history.

Winter Haven, Florida, is thirty-two miles southeast of Walt Disney World. Legoland Florida is built on the site of the former Cypress Gardens. These botanical gardens welcomed visitors from 1936 to 2009. Cypress Gardens was famous for its spectacular gardens, waterski show, and strolling southern belles in enormous hoopskirts. Legoland has preserved the botanical gardens and the waterski show. As an ode to history, Legoland recreated the famous southern belles as statues made entirely of Legos.

The preserved botanical gardens are worth a visit and cover thirty-nine acres of the park. It's a tropical paradise, complete with one legendary banyan tree that's as big as most homes. The tree was planted in a five-gallon bucket when Cypress Gardens opened in the 1930s.

There is a Florida theme park legend that somewhere inside these botanical gardens there is hidden a special tree. This tree, the only one left of its kind, secretes a key ingredient for the perfume Chanel #5. Supposedly, only one employee of Cypress Gardens (aka Legoland) knows the correct tree and is responsible for secretly obtaining the secretions. I have no idea if this is true, but it sure makes for a good story.

Oh, yeah, there are Legos here! Lots and lots of Legos. Walking around the park, you can find hundreds of structures—large and small—made from the famous plastic bricks. The most impressive displays include cityscapes from American cities. The fabulous Las Vegas strip made entirely of Legos is fun to study. There are many building zones where kids of all ages can try out their creativity. (A word of advice for all: It's a good idea to wash your hand thoroughly after playing with communal Legos.)

There are a lot of rides at Legoland, but the focus of these is on children aged two to seven. If you have children in that age range, then you can easily spend an entire day riding away at Legoland. If your children are older, you will spend about half a day looking at the displays.

The park is full of Lego-themed foods and shopping opportunities. For Lego enthusiasts, there are special Lego sets and mini-figures that can only be purchased inside the theme park.

Legoland Florida includes a hotel and water park on its property. Many citizens of Winter Haven were quite stressed when Cypress Gardens closed in 2009. The community lost a major source of jobs and revenue. The town breathed a collective sigh of relief when Legoland acquired the property, especially since

Legoland has more than doubled the scope of the old Cypress Gardens.

There is a great lesson for us all to learn from the story of Legoland Florida. This theme park took a vintage property popular with the Depends crowd and turned it into a modern zone for the Pampers crowd! All kidding aside, it's great when a theme park can create for the future while preserving parts of its past.

Reason #12:

Theme parks provide a rush of adrenaline in a legal, only mildly addicting way.

I get the shakes sometimes. If it has been too long since I've been inside a theme park, I start to get irritable and cranky. I know there are those of you out there who understand.

As I'm driving down the highway, I spot the first sign telling me which exit to take. Any green interstate sign with a theme park written on it makes me very excited. I start to breathe deeper with anticipation. The whole process of approaching the park feels like Christmas morning to me. I'm always glad when I've paid and I'm allowed past the parking booths—I feel like I've made the cut and get to enter. As I drive toward my parking spot, I feel a glow deep inside of me. Sometimes, it feels like that glow will creep up my throat and seep out of my face. (Yeah, that sounds gross. But it's the glow of anticipation! It's not snot.)

When I leave my car, I do a quick check that I've got everything I need in my special theme park satchel. Then I walk toward the entrance gate. I'm always smiling at this point. I relish the ritual of gaining admission and entering the park. If I've traveled any distance, or if it's a new park for me, all these feelings are heightened.

For my nineteen-year-old nephew, the experience is different. He is completely and utterly addicted to roller coasters. The highway sign just stresses him out—he doesn't start to feel the glow until he sees the highest drop of the tallest coaster in the park. With each drop he can spot, the glow strengthens. For him, the entrance ritual is just an obstacle to accomplish. As he waits in his first line, he goes into this odd state of suspended animation. I think it's his body's way of dealing with anticipation. Then, finally, he boards the coaster and rises above the park. Now he, too, can finally breathe.

Theme parks are an addiction, and my nephew and I have it bad. I used to feel inferior, and maybe even guilty, for having this addiction. But then my psychiatrist husband reminded me of all the much worse things I could be addicted to.

I could never be a drug addict because I don't even like the way that cough syrup makes me feel. I don't smoke anything, and I rarely drink. I like gambling at a slot machine—for about ten minutes—but then I start to think about how many books I had to sell to fund each pull, and the enjoyment stops. Since I've worn the same jeans, T-shirt, and hoodie for the last four years, nobody can accuse me of being a shopaholic. Theme parks are my vice.

But just as with any other addiction, there can be some negative aspects to craving themed entertainment. One of them is money. My addiction can be one expensive habit. I'm always aware of this and take several precautions. My husband and I have a strict theme park budget that we never deviate from. Both of us realize that theme parks come after, not before, the necessities of life. They come after not only what it costs us to live now, but also fully funding our plans for retirement.

Another negative aspect of theme-itis can be time. As much as I like to preach that theme park fantasy is my reality, I realize that the outside world is infinitely more important. Theme parks are my escape—they are not my replacement. Thankfully, I've been able to manage the negative aspects of loving theme parks.

I'm grateful that theme parks are legal. Otherwise, I'd have a real problem. I can imagine my nephew and me sneaking off to a remote corner of the countryside. There, we run through a clandestine forest with our theme park satchels hanging around us. With every noise, we stop in our tracks. We turn, hoping against hope that the theme park police have not spotted us. Continuing on, we see the forbidden gates ahead of us, and we run faster. Then we notice that vicious dogs have alerted the authorities to our presence. The dogs race toward us.

My nephew yells, "Drop your satchel!"

I reply, "I need my sunscreen!"

Finally, we reach the gates and throw our tickets at the attendant as we dash through. The dogs also make it through, but as soon as they pass inside the park, they turn into adorable puppies that spring into our arms for a hug.

We humans are such odd creatures. The same bodily function can feel different in two situations. The adrenaline rush felt after fleeing the police is horrible and unpleasant. But that same adrenaline feels wonderful and exhilarating while riding a roller coaster. I hope that I will never experience a world of forbidden theme parks so that I can continue my obsession with this healthy vice.

Dreamlly's Theme Park Recommendation

Six Flags
Various Locations in North America

When it comes to adrenaline, Six Flags packs quite a punch. Based on the number of properties, Six Flags is the largest theme park company in the world, with twenty parks. (Based on attendance, Six Flags ranks sixth.) Since many of the parks are similar, I've chosen to highlight the company as a whole.

Many people wonder, where does the name Six Flags come from? All right, perhaps many people don't go around wondering about Six Flags all day, but still, it's a curious name. Disneyland opened in 1955 with unprecedented media coverage, but the business community at the time couldn't care less. That all changed in 1956, when Disneyland's first financial reports were released and business-minded heads exploded all over the country. Disneyland was not just a media sensation; it was making a boatload of money.

A group of investors in Texas wanted a part of all that action. In 1961, they opened a Texas-themed park between Dallas and Fort Worth. The park was called Six Flags over Texas, in honor of the six nations that have governed Texas in the modern age: France, Mexico, Spain, the Republic of Texas, the Confederate States of America, and the United States of America. When the park opened, different themed lands represented each of the six flags.

When rumors flew around in the mid-1960s that Walt Disney was looking for a second location, the Texas investors also thought they'd better look to expand. (They weren't going to let Uncle Walt get ahead of them again.) They opened Six Flags over Georgia, near Atlanta, in 1967 and Six Flags over Mid-America, near St. Louis, in 1971. The name stuck, even though Georgia and Missouri have nothing to do with six flags. (Unless you count the McDonald's restaurant flag, of which both cities have way more than six.)

These three parks are the only ones in the collection that Six Flags built themselves. Since 1971, Six Flags has purchased existing theme parks and added them to their company. The major Six Flags parks are located near New York City/Philadelphia, Chicago, St. Louis, Dallas, San Antonio, Boston, Atlanta, Los Angeles, San Francisco, and Mexico City. Six Flags Hurricane Harbor, the company's chain of water parks, can be found either in or near most of their major locations.

Six Flags New Orleans was damaged beyond repair by Hurricane Katrina. This park was given to the city after a complicated court battle. Anything salvageable was auctioned, and the site abandoned. (Part of the mega-hit film *Jurassic World* was filmed here.)

Since its aggressive expansion began, Six Flags has moved away from Walt Disney's concept of themed lands. Most of the Six Flags parks could fall into the category of iron parks, since their focus is on rides and not theming. Still, instead of lands, many of the individual rides are highly themed attractions in themselves—most using characters from the world of DC Comics.

Let's talk about the adrenaline. Kingda Ka, the tallest roller coaster in the world, is located at Six Flags Great Adventure in New Jersey. It towers 456 feet above the Garden State. The third-tallest coaster is Superman: Escape from Krypton at Six Flags Magic Mountain in California. It stands at a mere 415 feet.

The two tallest wooden coasters in the United States are also at Six Flags parks. These are El Toro (181 feet) at Six Flags Great Adventure in New Jersey, and Goliath (165 feet) at Six Flags Great America outside Chicago. Goliath also holds the record for the longest wooden coaster drop of 180 feet. (How can a hill that's 165 feet tall have a drop that's 180 feet? You'll have to dig up the research on this one.)

Six Flags Magic Mountain, just north of Los Angeles, has no fewer than nineteen roller coasters. It's the current world record holder for number of coasters. Six Flags Great Adventure in New Jersey only has fourteen. (However, the park in New Jersey has the world's tallest, so perhaps they are even.)

But roller coasters aren't the only source of adrenaline on the planet. Zumanjaro at Six Flags Great Adventure in New Jersey is the world's tallest drop tower. This ride drops riders 415 feet. The second-tallest drop tower in the world is at Six Flags Magic Mountain and includes a four-hundred-foot drop. The two tallest swing carousel rides in the world are at Six Flags over Texas and Six Flags New England. They both stand at four hundred feet tall.

Of course, there are plenty of less adrenaline-filled rides at all the Six Flags properties. These are all world-class theme parks with plenty of attractions to keep you busy for an entire day. There are lots of shows and fantastic children's areas at each of the Six Flags locations. Oh, and there's also a lot of food inside these parks—and that brings on a whole different kind of adrenaline rush.

Reason #13:

Patience is a virtue; theme parks offer plenty of opportunities to attain it.

Some people like black licorice. Some people like poetry. There are even some people who like going to the dentist. But nobody likes waiting. It seems to take only about 1.6 seconds for me to eat an entire cake. But waiting for my suitcase at the airport seems to take at least three weeks.

My grandpa, before he left us to visit that big theme park in the sky, used to spend hours sitting on benches. I'd sit with him for a few minutes before I'd get antsy and run off to do something. I used to admire his patience. Then I learned that patience isn't just something you're born with. Patience is like playing the piano: it's a developed trait that requires practice.

There are two virtues of patience. The first is the ability to occupy your own brain without outside stimulus for a period of time. When I was younger, I used to have the same daydream as I waited in line for a roller coaster. I'd imagine that the coaster was actually an outer-space transit system that would whisk me at light speed to a planet far away. One of my favorite brain activities was to make up stories for all the "passengers" in front of me. I'd try to imagine where in the galaxy the people were traveling, and why. Which of these people were going to vacation on Saturn? Which were visiting family across Ursa Major? And which of them were up to some evil plot?

The second virtue of patience is the recognition that there are other people on the planet. I sometimes hear from people in my extended family who don't like theme parks. They hate theme parks because, they say, the parks are too crowded. I suspect that what they really don't like is knowing that the Earth isn't entirely comprised of their small house in their small town. There are billions of people on this planet, and it's healthy to see them. (Although, on a hot day, it may not be healthy to smell them.) It's also interesting to note that none of my relatives who hate theme parks have ever actually been to one.

I know what some of you analytic readers are thinking. The virtue of occupying your own brain has been replaced with smartphones. And the virtue of waiting for other people has been replaced with the ability to pay a theme park to skip the lines. Yes, both of these things are true, and I'll admit they cheapen the virtue of patience. However, a smartphone isn't going to make time go faster when you're waiting for news of a loved one's major surgery. No amount of money is going to allow you to live forever. At some point, you will be left with your own mind and the realization that we are all in the same boat.

There are a couple of theme park advancements that impact the way we wait in a line. In the late 1990s, Disney started constructing queues that are almost as amazing as the attractions themselves. Other parks started to follow the same trend. You no longer wait by a rope for ninety minutes until it's your turn to ride Peter Pan's Flight at the Magic Kingdom in Orlando. Now, you wander around the Darlings' house and look at all their cool British stuff.

There are some theme parks that have gotten rid of lines all together. At the famous Dumbo ride, again in the Magic Kingdom, guests are given pagers that vibrate when it's time to ride. In the meantime, kids can play inside a giant circus-themed playground. Universal Orlando's new Volcano Bay water theme park utilizes a completely line-free system that's based on a wristband. More of these systems will replace queues at theme parks. Remember, the businesspeople know you can't spend money on snacks and souvenirs if you're waiting in line.

There is this old adage: Good things come to those who wait. I believe that good things come to those who know *how* to wait. Brains need exercise, and theme park lines provide the perfect opportunity to just do nothing but think. But don't think about the work that's waiting for you at home. Instead, try to create stories about those waiting around you. (It's okay to be quite judgmental of strangers as long as you don't tell them about it.) There are also plenty of things you can count. Or, you can perform a scientific study: How many average people in a theme park line wear sneakers as opposed to flip-flops?

When my husband and I have a long layover at an airport, we are often desperate to escape the boredom. We search the arrivals screen for any flights coming from Orlando. As we head to the gate, we wager with each other over how many Disney shopping bags the arriving passengers will be carrying. There is a bit of science to this. We each secretly use our phones to discover what kind of aircraft is arriving and how many seats it contains. Time of day is also an important factor. In the morning, many vacationers will have gone right from the hotel to the airport— their purchased items are all safety packed. However, as the day goes on, vacationers will have tried to get in one more day at a theme park before heading to the Orlando airport. These passengers are much more likely to be carrying Disney bags that they didn't have the opportunity to pack. You can try this activity at any gate. How many Phillies or Eagles hats will the arriving flight from Philadelphia have? How many with hangovers will stumble their way off the flight from Las Vegas?

Will Rogers said, "The older we get, the fewer things seem worth waiting in line for." These words are so true, and I embrace them fully. I'm at the point in my life when I'm only going to wait for an extraordinary attraction that I've never experienced before. I'm not waiting even thirty minutes to ride the High Roller at Valleyfair. Instead, I'll find a nice bench in the shade, and I'll make no apologies about that.

Dreamlly's Theme Park Recommendation

Universal's Islands of Adventure
Orlando, Florida

I chose Universal's Islands of Adventure in Florida to represent the virtue of waiting in line. Please don't let that stop you from visiting. Yes, we'll talk about how long the lines can be. But we'll also talk about the incredible theming and general gorgeousness of this property.

When the Wizarding World of Harry Potter opened at Islands of Adventure, it was not uncommon for guests to wait up to four hours—just to enter the land. The lines for the individual attractions were considerably longer. Thankfully, the opening hype has passed, and things are much more manageable. But while guests can now just walk right into the land, lines for the main attractions can still last multiple hours.

There are two theme parks located at Universal Studios Resort Orlando: Universal Studios and Islands of Adventure. While both parks are world class, with plenty of awesome attractions, Islands of Adventure has better theming and is generally more beautiful.

The Wizarding World of Harry Potter actually exists in both parks. Islands of Adventure contains Hogsmeade, the village just outside Harry's school, Hogwarts. Diagon Alley, a wizard shopping district within London, is located at Universal Studios. The famous Hogwarts Express locomotive transports guests between the two separate sections of Harry's world. The Hogwarts Express is a fantastic attraction where every inch was thought about and themed to perfection. Riders take a story-filled trip through the English countryside. However, in order to ride the Hogwarts Express, you must have a ticket that allows you entry to both theme parks. (Oh, those clever businesspeople.)

Hogwarts Castle rises high above Islands of Adventure. Not only is it a great photo opportunity, but it holds a spectacular attraction: Harry Potter and the Forbidden Journey. This attraction contains a little bit of everything, from screen simulators to animatronics, all while sitting on a magical bench that moves in every way possible. The queue for this attraction is as good as the ride itself. You'll wind your way through Hogwarts castle and see all the places where the students spend their days. If you want to see the castle and don't want to ride, there is a very nice waiting room where you can sit while others in your party journey with Harry.

The rest of the Wizarding World of Harry Potter includes more rides and all the shops that offer merchandise for the discerning witch, wizard, or muggle among us. Of course, the wand shop is the most visited. And in true theme park style, if you purchase a wand, you can use it to perform all kinds of interactive magic throughout the land.

All foods mentioned in the Harry Potter books can be found somewhere at the Wizarding World of Harry Potter. The famous butterbeer is sold regular or frozen; it's quite refreshing on a hot day. The chocolate frogs mentioned in the first book of the series are available, along with every kind of cake, cookie, and ice cream imaginable.

Harry has a huge presence at Islands of Adventure, but there is a lot more. The rest of the park winds around a central lake. Skull Island: Reign of Kong is an immersive ride through the world of the giant ape. Jurassic Park includes a water ride that provides close-up views of various dinosaurs. The large thrill rides of Island of Adventure lie in Marvel Super Hero Island. (Even though Disney owns Marvel, they must honor a theme park licensing agreement made before Mickey bought Captain America.)

My favorite land at Islands of Adventure is Seuss Landing. This is the children's section of the park, but it's just as good for me too. There are no straight lines in Seuss Landing, and everything is as colorful as the immortal books of Dr. Seuss. The Caro-Seuss-el rotates with every kind of—well—thing imaginable. The High in the Sky Seuss Trolley Train Ride is my first ride any time I visit the park. There is a Cat in the Hat attraction, and you can see the place where the Lorax pinched his butt and flew off to wherever Loraxes fly off to when they pinch their butts (you'll have to read the book to understand this one). You can get green eggs and ham at a small outdoor stand, or you can dine inside the enormous Circus McGurkus Café Stoo-pendous.

In addition to all this, the Universal Studios property includes a water theme park called Volcano Bay. There are six on-site hotels for all types of budgets. A giant shopping and dining district called City Walk completes the resort.

Reason #14:

Creativity is an admired human trait that theme parks exemplify.

I love working with kids because they are just so darn creative. Ask a group of kids to draw their future houses and you'll get all sorts of wonderful creations. Unencumbered by experience and expectation, kids use few straight lines in their work. Do you want a swimming pool in your living room? A four-year-old can make that happen. How about a kitchen that's up in a tower? No problem for a third grader. Interested in a slide instead of stairs? That can be done.

With all this potential creativity born into us, why do all our neighborhoods look so similar? Why don't we have spiral slides between floors? It's really not that hard to design a hidden room located behind a sliding bookcase—why do none of us have one? There are so many straight lines all over residential areas. Why? I suspect it has less to do with finances and more to do with our obsession with pretending to be grown-ups.

Theme parks not only allow creativity, but insist upon it. Creativity comes in both macro and micro forms. Certainly, the big picture of overall theme is important. However, it's often those little micro-moments of creativity that keep us coming back and wanting more.

Mickey's Philharmagic is a fantastic 4-D film at Walt Disney World, Tokyo Disneyland, and Hong Kong Disneyland. It's one of my all-time favorite attractions because its story is centered around Donald Duck, and I have a soft spot for that quite human duck. At the conclusion of the film, Donald is shot out of a tuba and sent flying through the air. If that were how the attraction ended, it would still be great. However, those famous Disney Imagineers with their wonderful creativity always go the extra mile. The attraction really ends with the audience turning to see a hole where Donald has just hit the back wall. His butt and feet (no pants, of course) are still sticking out of the smoking hole. Now, this is creativity!

The Wizarding World of Harry Potter is found within Universal parks in Orlando, Hollywood, and Japan. It's an all-out creative extravaganza. At the entrance to this themed land, there is sign stating, "Please respect the spell limits." It is such a small detail, but its creative impact is enormous. This sign subtly signals us that an incredible amount of thought went into the creation of Harry's world. The sign for The Leaky Cauldron, a wizard tavern, actually leaks. If you pick up the themed phone inside the land's massive King's Cross train station and dial 62442 (magic), the Ministry of Magic will answer. Moaning Myrtle, a ghost who haunts restrooms in the Harry Potter books, also haunts the restrooms in the theme parks.

The Tilt-A-Whirl ride at Holiday World is located in its Thanksgiving section. However, in true theme park style, the riders sit inside a turkey as they whirl around. At Hersheypark, near the famous chocolate factory in Pennsylvania, there is a ride themed all around Reese's Peanut Butter Cups. While at Camp

Snoopy within Knott's Berry Farm in California, kids can try to stay clean while riding Pig Pen's Mud Buggies.

As you wait to ride Dinosaur! at Disney's Animal Kingdom in Florida, you'll wander through an industrial laboratory. There are three pipes running above you with chemical compounds listed on them. Your high school chemistry teacher would be able to tell you that the chemicals listed on the red pipe are the ingredients for ketchup. The yellow pipe contains the chemical recipe for mustard. And the white pipe? Mix the chemicals with the last two ingredients—CH_3COOH (vinegar) and $C_6H_{12}O_6$ (sugar)—and you'll have mayonnaise.

It's not just the designers and builders that are in on the creativity. It's also the park employees. It is always shocking to me that there are people who don't know the difference between Disneyland and Walt Disney World. (I tell my nephews and niece that these are the people you don't want to marry.) Anyway, without getting into too much detail, the famous Disney castle in Disneyland is much smaller than the one in Walt Disney World. I had been to Walt Disney World in Florida many times before I traveled to its older sister, Disneyland, in California. During my first visit to Disneyland, I was standing in front of the castle when a cast member (Disneyspeak for employee) noticed my "first time visitor" button.

"It's your first time to Disneyland!" she said. "Welcome!"

"Yep," I answered, "I've been to Disney World many times, but this is my first time here."

"What do you think?" she asked me.

"It's beautiful. I love it. The only complaint I have is that the castle here is just too small."

"Oh, I know," she replied. "See, at Disney World, they have Cinderella Castle. Here, we have Sleeping Beauty Castle. Sleeping

Beauty is nice and all, but she spends all her time out in the forest with her woodland critters. She just doesn't need a big place because she loves to hang around outdoors. Cinderella, on the other hand, loves that big place in Florida with the cleaning she can do in there."

This conversation completely made my entire trip to California. The cast member I spoke with, a Disney photographer, exhibited unbelievable creativity. She engaged me in conversation and made me feel like I was part of the magic. In that moment, Sleeping Beauty and Cinderella were unquestionably real people who lived in these famous buildings.

Speaking of the Disney princesses, I can't imagine the kind of creativity it must take to portray one of these women. I've had many opportunities over the years to stand back and watch Disney princesses interact with children. No matter what the kids say—no matter what questions they ask—a true princess always has a quick and appropriate response. My niece and I chatted with Ariel one night just before dinner. As we left she said, "Have a nice dinner—just don't tell Sebastian if you order the crab!"

If you really want to experience human creativity in all its glory, then you must visit the special Halloween parties at either of the American Disney Parks. The decorations are amazing, and even the food is themed around the season. I've found that the Disney villains are even more creative than the princesses. Gaston and Cruella De Vil are always fun to chat with, if you can tolerate their egos. In addition, you'll observe the height of creativity when you notice the costumes that the Disney characters are wearing. (You can't get more creative than a costume wearing a costume.)

Creativity is the most exciting and inspirational force on the planet. What a world this would be if we'd all aspire to create something. Just avoid straight lines, and don't be afraid to put a swing set in your living room.

Dreamlly's Theme Park Recommendation

Tokyo DisneySea
Tokyo, Japan

If you get sick of hyperbole, then you'd better go and grab a motion discomfort bag. It's about to get real deep in here. But the fact is, there aren't enough adjectives available to describe Tokyo DisneySea, or what I like to call it: the most creative place on Earth.

The whole country of Japan is sort of like one big theme park. It's by far the cleanest country on the planet. The trains and other forms of futuristic transportation look like something out of Walt Disney's dreams. The people are polite, friendly, and helpful, as if they are all working at a giant theme park.

Tokyo Disneyland was the first international Disney Park. The Japanese culture combined with the Disney philosophy to make an incredible destination. Everything works at Tokyo Disneyland all the time. Some Japanese engineer won't be able to sleep at night if even just one of the many enchanted tiki birds isn't flapping properly. This park is thirty-five years old, and it looks as pristine as it did on day one.

In 2001, a second theme park opened next door to Tokyo Disneyland. It was the incredible and unbelievable Tokyo

DisneySea. Disneyland presents themed lands that immerse the guests in stories. DisneySea presents themed ports of call that tell the stories. From the second you depart the Tokyo Disney Resort monorail, you are immersed in an intricate story that keeps getting better and better as your day unfolds. You won't want the story to end—I never do and usually have to be dragged out of the park by security.

Your adventure will start by the Aquasphere, an enormous globe that depicts the planet in all its glory. The globe is covered with streams of running water as it spins lightly on its base. It's clear that the real theme of DisneySea is travel.

The entrance to the actual park is underneath the amazing Hotel Mira Costa—the only Disney hotel in the world that is completely inside a theme park. You will notice that you've not only traveled in distance but also in time as you find yourself in the middle of the Italian Renaissance. Mediterranean Harbor is the first port of call.

Much like Main Street, USA, over at Disneyland, Mediterranean Harbor is full of shops and restaurants. However, there is also a ginormous body of water. There are no parades here; instead, spectacles worthy of ancient Rome are played out on this water. These are huge extravaganzas full of ships, fountains, fire, pyrotechnics, Disney characters, kites, jet skis, stunts, music, and enough goosebumps to make you think that you've got chicken pox.

The center of Tokyo DisneySea is Mount Prometheus, an enormous volcano that rises just beyond Mediterranean Harbor. This volcano erupts with the power of jet engines from time to time and also plays an important role in all of DisneySea's elaborate water shows. Mount Prometheus conceals a ride: Journey to the Center of the Earth. In fact, all the attractions in this area of the park, known as Mysterious Island, come from the work of Jules Verne. You'll find that 20,000 Leagues under the Sea is a ride unlike anything else you've ever experienced. (It's not anything like the walk-through version at Disneyland Paris.)

It may seem odd to you that I can name a favorite attraction. How could I choose one from among the thousands of attractions around the globe? Well, out of all the attractions in all of the theme parks on Earth, nothing fills my soul with as much joy as Sindbad's Storybook Voyage. (It's not a typo; the Japanese put an extra letter in Sindbad.) This boat ride, located in the Arabian Coast section of the park, is an absolute dream. You'll follow Sindbad and his delightful tiger companion Chandu on a journey to follow the compass of their hearts. Along the way, they help a multitude of those in need and discover the treasure of their dreams. Hundreds of audio-animatronics perform seamlessly with music, and some of the animatronics even sing in harmony with each other. Sindbad's Storybook Voyage is truly an escape. On this ride, it's impossible to think about anything else except the splendor of it all.

I'm not even one quarter of the way around the park yet, so I'll speed it up. Mermaid Lagoon is an over-the-top children's area themed to *The Little Mermaid.* It's mostly indoors and makes a great place to escape the sometimes uncooperative Tokyo weather. Near the rear of the park, Lost River Delta contains the major thrill rides in an Amazon-like setting. Port Discovery is DisneySea's version of Tomorrowland. Nemo and Friends SeaRider, the park's newest attraction, is located here.

The last port for you to discover is American Waterfront. This is New York City in all its 1920s splendor. Tokyo's versions of the Tower of Terror and Toy Story Mania can be found here. But the real star of American Waterfront is the S.S. *Columbia,* a full-size ocean liner that's open for you to explore. For the best view in the park, climb to the highest deck of the S.S. *Columbia* at sunset and look toward the front of the ship. On a clear day, you will see the stunning form of Mt. Fuji. During certain times of the year, the moon will rise from behind Mr. Fuji. You will probably cry if you see this.

Part of the charm of Tokyo DisneySea is that it's located right on the real Pacific Ocean. There was no need to construct any elaborate berm to divide the park from the outside world. Nothing could complement DisneySea more than a real sea— I'm so glad that the Disney Imagineers welcomed the beautiful Pacific into this fantasy dreamworld.

You'll see a lot of Duffy at Tokyo DisneySea. Duffy is this adorable stuffed bear that Minnie made for Mickey so that he wouldn't get lonely on all his travels. Duffy is huge here, and fans line up for hours to get a chance to buy Duffy-related merchandise. (I'm not kidding—hours.) Over the years, Duffy has picked up a girlfriend, as traveling stuffed bears are apt to do. Her name is Shellie Mae. She is also a bear because Disney discourages cross-species dating. (Except, why did Goofy date Clarabelle the cow? Everyone knows that Clarabelle is much more suited for Horace Horsecollar.) Anyway, Duffy also has a cat friend named Gelatoni and a bunny friend named Stella Lou.

Aside from DisneySea and Disneyland, Tokyo Disney Resort includes four Disney hotels, a host of partner hotels, and a train station with a short fifteen-minute connection to the main Tokyo Station. Ikspiari, a large shopping and dining district, is also located on the property. Ikspiari is mostly covered and climate-controlled for your enjoyment.

At the end of the night, after you've seen whatever incredible show was presented in the harbor, you'll have to force yourself to leave. It's as difficult as it is to wake up in the morning and go to work. Since the beginning of humanity, we have used stories to entertain, to convey information, and to generally escape. Tokyo DisneySea is my happy place because it tells its stories so extremely well. The purpose of creativity is for us to be inspired to learn about ourselves by interacting with things outside of us. What could I, a plain guy from a small Minnesota town, possibly have to learn from an Arabian puppet and his pet tiger? Well, as it turns out, an awful lot.

Reason #15:

Theme parks force people to exercise.

What's worse: waiting in line or exercising? Probably exercising. At least while you're waiting in line, you can snack on some popcorn. I'm one of those people who needs to be tricked into exercising. Nothing is better at tricking me to do anything than the theme park industry.

Thrill Laboratory, a group of scientists in Britain that like theme parks, recently completed a study about roller coasters and energy. It turns out that the average person burns seventy calories just by riding a coaster for two minutes. It all has to do with adrenaline production and certain muscles that you tense as you ride. But for all intents and purposes, all you had to do to burn these seventy calories was to sit on your butt.

Now, I won't spoil anyone's fun by stating how many calories are in a funnel cake. However, it's a heck of a lot more than seventy. Fortunately, by design, theme parks are sprawling places with equally sprawling parking lots. Walking is a fantastic way to exercise.

I was curious as to how much we walked during a recent visit to Walt Disney World. My husband wore one of those fitness trackers. During the four days of theme park visits, we never walked less than twenty thousand steps in one day. According to Google, twenty thousand steps is around 7.58 miles. Our longest day, when we visited two parks and went to Mickey's Not So Scary Halloween Party, gave us just over thirty thousand steps. Google says that's 11.36 miles. In four days, we walked 35.21 miles. As a general rule, a 180-pound person burns one hundred calories per mile. We were able to burn an entire day of eating just by walking and having fun for four days. This doesn't include the calories we burned by existing the rest of the time when we weren't inside a theme park.

The great thing about theme park walking is that it doesn't seem like exercise at all. Not only is there a lot to look at, but there are instant rewards. At the end of a theme park walk, you get to go on a ride! I detest walking on a treadmill. It'd be so much easier if I knew that when I finished, I'd get to sit in the air-conditioned comfort of Walt Disney's Enchanted Tiki Room. I can't imagine how miserable I would be if my car broke down at the grocery store and I had to walk 11.36 miles to get home. But at Walt Disney World, 11.36 miles seemed like nothing at all.

If you visit a water theme park, then your amount of exercise really shoots up. Just by nature, it takes a lot of energy to play in the water. A 180-pound person burns about three hundred calories for every thirty minutes of swimming. Now, I don't know about you, but staying afloat in a wave pool is a lot harder than swimming laps—and it's easy to lose track of time while having fun.

The reason we exercise is so that we can be healthy enough to enjoy the planet, each other, and ourselves. It's fantastic when the exercise itself involves enjoying the planet, each other, and ourselves.

**Dreamlly's
Theme Park
Recommendation**

Epcot
Walt Disney World, Florida

The largest theme park in the world is Disney's Animal Kingdom at Walt Disney World in Florida. But it's not the park that offers the most walking. Most of Animal Kingdom's vast acreage is reserved for the animals. The theme park in Orlando that offers the most exercise is Epcot. It's a 1.25-mile walk around the World Showcase at Epcot, and that's only one portion of the park—it's also not counting any steps you take to visit the themed countries along the way.

Walt Disney created the acronym EPCOT to stand for Experimental Prototype Community of Tomorrow. His plans for this community were quite different from what it became. Walt envisioned an actual town and had all sorts of interesting plans for the daily operation of such a town. After his death in 1966, the Walt Disney Company went on to build the Magic Kingdom. Now that they had plenty of space for once, the businesspeople decided that a second park would entice guests to stay longer on Disney property. The complexity of building an actual city was too great, and Walt's idea turned into a single theme park. In 1982, EPCOT Center opened to the public. (It had lost its acronym.) In 1994, EPCOT Center was rebranded as Epcot. (It had lost its capitalism.)

Although the original scope is changing, Epcot remains sort of a permanent world's fair. The first half of the park, Future World, is meant to showcase human interaction with various aspects of a progressive society. The second half of the park is World Showcase. This portion of the park includes recreations of eleven countries around the World Showcase Lagoon.

Future World is changing. It used to incorporate the principles of what Walt Disney called "edutainment." However, in recent years, it's become more focused on the *tainment* and less on the *edu*. Still, there are some amazing attractions to experience in Future World.

The centerpiece of Epcot is its iconic geodesic dome called Spaceship Earth. This structural sphere is home to an original Epcot attraction of the same name. While on Spaceship Earth, passengers travel back in time to learn about the history of communication. The story is told through animatronics and individual screens located in front of each pair of seats. The fact that Spaceship Earth has been running since 1982 is a testament to its quality.

The most popular attraction in Future World is Soarin'. This flight simulator takes guests on an aerial tour as they sit in a robotic hang glider that moves along with a massive screen. Soarin' is okay. It's located in a pavilion called the Land, along with an educational boat ride. I find that the boat ride is a much better attraction. On Living with the Land, guests ride in boats to learn about humanity's interaction with various ecosystems. Then the boats take a tour of Disney's greenhouses, where food is grown in innovative ways. The food produced in these houses is actually served at Walt Disney World restaurants.

If you like manatees, you can visit them at the Seas pavilion. After riding the Seas with Nemo and Friends, you can view manatees in one of the largest aquariums on Earth. This pavilion also holds dolphins, sharks, and lots of tropical fish.

Across Future World, you'll find Mission: Space. This nausea-inducing pukefest was the first theme park ride to provide guests with motion discomfort bags—I'm totally not joking about that! The Epcot janitors must have gotten tired of cleaning up all that vomit because guests can now choose a version of the ride that's less violent.

The last of the major Future World attractions is Test Track. Here, guests ride a test car through a series of mock experiments. You'll see how well your car holds up in the heat and cold. You'll do some quick stops and travel on some bumpy roads. Then your car will take a speed test around the pavilion. While waiting in the queue, you design a virtual car that gets tested along with your real ride vehicle.

As you walk around Future World, you'll notice the enormous World Showcase spreading out around the lagoon. This is where you can really work off any bad food choices you've made. The World Showcase is Disney at its finest, and you'll want to spend a lot of time meandering through each of the countries. Some have attractions, some have films, some have displays—but they all have lots and lots of food!

In recent years, there has been this word-of-mouth activity for adults that involves getting a drink in each country. Just be advised: Eleven drinks are a lot to handle, and not cheap. But as the evening goes on, you'll see some adults partaking in this ritual. Later, in the parking lot, you may see some adults regretting this ritual.

Working clockwise, the first country is Mexico. Mexico contains the only Donald Duck ride on the planet and is always a favorite stop for me. (Donald is one of the Three Caballeros and is quite popular in Spanish-speaking countries.) Mexico holds my favorite of Epcot's restaurants: the San Angel Inn.

Norway used to attract eight visitors each day. Then a little film called *Frozen* came out. Norway now holds a *Frozen* attraction that is part boat ride and part log flume. (It uses the same track as the previous Maelstrom ride, if you're familiar with that.)

China hosts a wonderful film called *Reflections of China*. This is the most informative of Epcot's country-based films. The theater is large and really well air-conditioned. Also, Chinese acrobats perform regularly in this space.

Germany at Epcot is famous for its lively beer hall—and this country has the best chocolate in the park. There is also a shop that sells imported nutcrackers and all sorts of wonderful items for *Weihnachten* (Christmas).

Italy doesn't have an attraction. Instead, it has pizza! Really good pizza! You will need an advance reservation to eat at Via Napoli, but it's worth it. The pizzas are baked in three brick ovens that are named after Italy's three active volcanos: Etna, Vesuvius, and Stromboli. (Stromboli, the mountain, came before Stromboli, a villain in *Pinocchio*.)

The United States is represented by the American Adventure pavilion. This building hosts a show that presents the history of the country. The show uses film, music, and the best audio-animatronics that Disney has ever produced. It's an incredible experience that's updated to reflect modern history. But be advised, this is not the rose-colored history of America you may have learned in school. You'll see slavery, hear from Chief Joseph about the treatment of Native Americans, learn about women's suffrage, and see AIDS patients turned away from hospitals. Still, this journey, narrated by animatronic Ben Franklin and Mark Twain, strives to explain the events that shaped the USA.

Unfortunately, there isn't any decent food in the United States pavilion. It's quite sad that Disney hasn't found a way to present the extraordinary diversity of our country's cuisine. (I vote for a buffet with one item from each state! Minnesota's contribution will be hotdish.)

Food is not lacking in Japan. There are several restaurants here and lots of seafood. Japanland also includes a Japanese department store with all its kitschy wonders.

The Moroccan pavilion is the most intricate, with many winding pathways decorated beautifully with tiles. There are many shops here, and the fantastic smell of food wafts all around the area. Spices are a popular item for sale, as are rugs.

France has fantastic food and a film. *Impressions de France* is presented throughout the day. It's more of a surreal depiction of the country and less informative. France will be getting an attraction based on the Pixar film *Ratatouille* in the near future. An authentic French patisserie, Les Halles, is a popular place for pastries and breads.

The United Kingdom is represented with fish and chips and soccer. The shops contain lots of items related to *Dr. Who*, *Downton Abbey*, Paddington Bear, and the Beatles. There is also a tea shop.

Canada hosts the funniest of the Epcot films: *O, Canada!* It's narrated by Martin Short. On a hot day, watching the Canadian landscape in the air-conditioned theater is a real treat! Le Cellier is a Canadian steakhouse and one of the most difficult reservations to get. There is also a store dedicated entirely to Canada's national sport: sunbathing. (Just kidding—the store is dedicated to hockey.)

Many theme park enthusiasts consider Epcot's nighttime show to be the best theme park show in history. *Illuminations:*

Reflections of Earth is presented around the World Showcase Lagoon each night. It is quite spectacular, but I'll keep my opinion to myself with regard to whether it's the best in history. Still, this show uses all the nighttime magic that the Imagineers wield so well.

The whole point of writing this section was to prove that Epcot is enormous. By the time you've walked the whole park and strolled around each of the countries, you'll be ready for a nice long rest. Just please, don't cheat. There are some boats that ferry passengers across the World Showcase Lagoon, but if you take the boat, you can't eat that extra Mickey-shaped brownie.

Reason #16:

Theme parks have even more history.

At the conclusion of the last installment of theme park history, the automobile had pretty much extinguished America's amusement park industry. This was almost the death of the entertainment park idea altogether. But then, some very smart people figured out that motorists liked to have a destination. Not only that, but the United States began to acquire a solid middle class. For the first time in history, the average family had disposable income. The time was right, and the old amusement parks gave way to our modern theme parks.

Two parks in the United States claim to be America's first theme park. Holiday World in Indiana and Knott's Berry Farm in southern California both claim this honor. In fact, I recently purchased shirts from both of these parks with "America's First Theme Park" written on them.

Holiday World opened as Santa Claus Land in 1946. Knott's Berry Farm began as a berry stand in 1920; however, Walter Knott didn't construct his themed Old West Town until sometime in the mid-1940s. Whichever one was first, both of these places took the idea of amusement parks to the next level. Whether through a replica of Santa's North Pole Village or an old mining town from days gone by, the creators of these parks wanted guests to step into a story.

One day in the late 1940s, Walter Knott added a steam locomotive that circled his park. He had a friend, also named Walter, who was an avid train enthusiast. Mr. Knott invited his friend, Mr. Disney, over for lunch and to ride his train. Walt Disney was probably thrilled as he rode the rails—and, perhaps, he was a bit jealous. The world of themed entertainment would never be the same after that moment.

While Walt Disney's wife Lillian claimed that amusement parks were dangerous and dirty, Walt forged ahead with plans to build his own park. On the back of a napkin, he drew his famous "hub and spoke" plan that included differently themed lands meeting in the middle—this design has endured through the ages. Walt wanted a place where adults and children could have fun together. He also wanted guests to be able to step inside his famous films.

The obstacles that presented themselves during the construction of Walt's park are the stuff of legend. This had never been done before. Existing parks of the era had all evolved slowly over time. Walt's park started as a clean slate: an orange grove in Anaheim, California. He needed to build everything in only one year's time. He also needed the money to do all this. But he was tenacious. More importantly, he had the genius business sense of his brother Roy to rely on.

July 17, 1955, is D-day for all theme park enthusiasts. Whatever you think about Disney as a corporation, however you feel for Walt Disney himself, and wherever you travel to find your own nostalgia—you must admit that Disneyland is a masterpiece that changed the world. Disneyland had one entrance and exit gate. This innovation alone was remarkable for the time. But

Disneyland was far more innovative than just the gate. Countless theme park ideas can be traced back to that day in 1955.

It took only three months for Walt Disney to welcome his one-millionth guest. When word of this got around, everyone started to scramble to build their own parks. Over the next two decades, every major metropolitan area in the United States claimed at least one such place. Now we have another first: competition.

Competition has been great for the theme park industry—it's what pushes the coasters higher and makes costumer service better. Disneyland opened and forced Knott's Berry Farm to expand. Universal Studios in Hollywood was tired of losing tourists to Anaheim and opened their own attractions. Consequently, Disneyland added more attractions, which forced Knott's Berry Farm to add roller coasters. Eventually, Walt Disney World opened in Florida. Nearby, a small park exclusively for the employees of the local brewery added some rides and started charging admission: Busch Gardens was born. SeaWorld soon followed, as did Universal Studios Orlando. Walt Disney World saw the competition and added three more theme parks to its property. And so on, and so on.

But the United States is certainly not the only country to enjoy a love affair with theme parks. During the American occupation of Japan in the post-World War II era, railroad companies were given subsidies to expand. The savvy Japanese railroad executives took a cue from an earlier American trend and built theme parks at the end of their tracks. Japan's theme parks took off in a big way, and there is no stopping them. In fact, the Japanese people's attraction to themed entertainment is unsurpassed anywhere on this planet. During the late twentieth century, theme parks spread throughout all of Asia. The continent of Asia contains three Disney Resorts: Tokyo, Hong Kong, and Shanghai. North America, the birthplace of Mickey Mouse, only has two Disney Resorts.

Europe continues to develop their own theme park culture. The venerable older parks are well preserved and offer a mix of history with modern thrills. Joining them are entirely new and fantastic parks that are complete with hotels, water parks, and world-class restaurants.

Today, the center of new theme park development lies in the Middle East. Both Dubai and Abu Dhabi have ambitious plans to construct several massive parks. The jury is still out on whether their economies can support these plans. There are also opposing beliefs about the feasibility of international tourism to this part of the world. We will have to stay tuned when it comes to the Middle East theme parks.

There you have it—from Xerxes to Marie Antoinette, world's fairs to "end of the line," and Disneyland to Shanghai Disneyland. Theme parks have a unique and fascinating history. Their futures will be just as fun to watch.

Dreamlly's Theme Park Recommendation

Holiday World
Santa Claus, Indiana

Holiday World, one of the two parks that claim to be America's first, is located in Santa Claus, Indiana. Yes, that's the real name of the town—the town is older than the park. When early settlers decided to incorporate their village, they weren't able to think of a name. The story (one that the town likes to tell) is that all the settlers were meeting in a church. Not one of them was able to contribute a likable name. Oh, and did I not mention … it was Christmas Eve. Suddenly, a wind blew across the prairie, and a faint sound of bells could be heard. A child exclaimed that it must be Santa Claus. The settlers all laughed; then looked at each other, and faster than you can say Kris Kringle—the town had been named.

Santa Claus is located in the far southern part of Indiana, seventy-three miles straight west of Louisville, Kentucky. It's a very small town, but don't let that fool you. Holiday World is a massive park with rides that are ranked among the best in the world. To see giant roller coasters rise out of nowhere in the middle of the prairie is a sight to behold. I was astonished the first time that I drove there, and you will be too.

Holiday World is divided into five themed areas: Christmas, Halloween, Fourth of July, Thanksgiving, and Splashin' Safari. Each area is well themed with attractions, shows, restaurants, and shops. Splashin' Safari is a world-class water park with the two longest water coasters on the planet.

Speaking of coasters, Holiday World is a major draw for roller coaster enthusiasts. Its massive wooden coaster, the Voyage, is consistently ranked as the best in the world. I've ridden it—it doesn't stop. The Voyage seems to take you through the woods to Kentucky and back. It's located in the Thanksgiving area of the park and is themed after the Pilgrims' fateful voyage on the Mayflower.

While visiting the Pilgrims in Thanksgivingland, don't miss the world's only Thanksgiving-themed dark ride. Here, guests ride around and attempt to use laser guns to shoot at turkeys. It's brilliant. (And for the vegetarian readers: Don't worry. The turkeys seem to escape, and at the ride's conclusion, you will see a family enjoying a nice Thanksgiving pizza.)

The best experience in the whole park is, beyond a doubt, Thanksgiving dinner at the Plymouth Rock Café. I can't put into words how great it feels to eat turkey and all the trimmings inside this air-conditioned haven during a hot July day. Just don't eat too much pumpkin pie, because Mrs. Claus has a bakery over in Christmasland.

Are you tired of theme parks that seem to "nickel and dime" you around every turn? Head to Holiday World for a new perspective. This theme park offers free parking! I know, I know, it's a hard concept for Americans to understand—so, I will explain it to you. At Holiday World, nobody pays to park a car. There aren't any toll booths. You just drive in and park, like you're at the grocery store! It's unbelievable! But, wait—there's more. Holiday World provides free sunscreen for all guests. And now, I've saved the best for last. Please sit down before you read this sentence because many have fainted upon hearing the news: Holiday World gives all guests unlimited free soda just for entering the park. That's right! Just head to one of the many beverage centers, grab a cup, and drink as much soda as you can handle.

As you can see, Holiday World is a special place. If I were to imagine a park that truly embodies the spirit of Santa Claus, it would look exactly like Holiday World.

Reason #17:

Theme parks offer a catalyst to discuss world events and social responsibility.

I've spent a lot of time writing about how theme parks offer an escape from the world. For 95 percent of my total theme park experiences, that's what they have been: an escape. But theme parks don't exist on a separate plane of reality. They are created by humans, operated by humans, and visited by humans. Unfortunately, humanity is not a species known for its ability to maintain harmonious environments. The other 5 percent of my theme park experience involves those times when the real world seeps in through the park gates.

In 2013, CNN produced a documentary called *Blackfish*. This film tells of the controversial treatment of killer whales at the SeaWorld parks. A death of a SeaWorld trainer in Orlando is also profiled in the documentary, as is SeaWorld's killer whale breeding program. Since the film's debut, SeaWorld's attendance has fallen dramatically. Consequently, SeaWorld has discontinued its killer whale breeding program and is phasing out live performances of these whales. SeaWorld in Orlando is constructing an enormous killer whale habitat to house its current population.

I, too, watched *Blackfish*. I watched it three times, and it is, indeed, quite upsetting. I was ready to throw in the towel when it came to SeaWorld. But then I heard respected zoologist Jack Hanna criticizing the film on *Anderson Cooper 360*. I decided to do some research on my own. Some of the trainers who participated in the documentary had no idea they were being edited to show only negative aspects—they assert that *Blackfish* is misleading and often incorrect. Other trainers who appear in the film had been fired by SeaWorld for inappropriate conduct well before any controversy began. One former SeaWorld trainer, and an outspoken critic of the park, was featured in a racist video where he uses the n-word several times. This same trainer was also caught in a lie when journalist John Stossel produced papers in 2015 proving that the trainer's tweets were deceitful.

Where is the truth? Which set of former trainers should we believe? On one side, there is a theme park corporation that ultimately needs to make money in order to exist. On the other side is a group of animal activists that ultimately need to make money in order to exist. As with most things, the truth is somewhere in the middle.

We live in a world that forces us to view everything like a killer whale—in black and white. Just remember that there are plenty of dolphins—shades of gray—around as well. Any rational person will question the humaneness of keeping such large animals in confined spaces. But rational people must also praise SeaWorld for its efforts to save marine life. SeaWorld funds the largest sea animal rehabilitation program of the planet. To date, they've saved more than twenty-five thousand animals.

Is it possible to fund the rescue programs without the revenue SeaWorld gets from guests paying to see the killer whales? Not a chance. As you see, there are no easy answers to this controversy. Each person has to decide whether or not to visit SeaWorld.

SeaWorld is far from the only park that finds itself mired in controversy. Due to their reputation and history, Disney Parks can never get a free pass. Any decision Mickey makes explodes onto social media, where it is discussed to death. A simple thing like the closing of a toilet will surely find its way through the headlines and into the posts of Disney chatrooms. Your local park can probably raise its prices without anyone noticing. When Disney raises the price of admission, the news seems to make a national crisis.

In recent months, the addition of Donald Trump to the Magic Kingdom's Hall of Presidents has sparked praise and outrage from all over the globe. In this case, the argument has left the Internet and is present inside the actual park as guests yell out comments during the presentation. Some think that Donald Trump should be in the Hall of Presidents, since he won the vote of the electoral college. Others believe that Donald Trump's politics and complete lack of decorum are destructive. There was no way Disney could win, and any decision they made was sure to offend a whole lot of people. (Perhaps we're at a place where the Hall of Presidents is no longer valid. An attraction that focuses on the public service of everyday citizens and less on the actions of wealthy politicians may be more in line with Walt Disney's original intent.)

Disney has also decided to "clean up" the classic Pirates of the Caribbean attraction. The classic version included a scene in which pirates were selling women; that scene has been removed in Paris and Florida. It will soon be removed at all Disney Parks.

There is a lot of alcohol at Universal Studio's Halloween Horror Nights on both coasts. A lot. Some people love it, and others think it has gotten way out of hand. Should Universal stop selling alcohol at this event? What if attendance falls because there is no liquor? What if attendance falls because there is lots of liquor? How can park employees tolerate the poor behavior of drunk guests? Keep in mind that lower attendance means fewer hours for theme park workers. Many Universal employees are involved in the sale of alcohol. If these employees are let go, they can't go to the grocery store in Orlando—they can't afford to drive to the Florida shore for an afternoon of fun. Theme parks have hard decisions to make that have real economic consequences.

The important thing we can do as theme park guests is to gather information, talk about it, and make the decision that is best for us. My nephews and niece are all old enough now that I can discuss controversy with them. Sometimes, we make a decision and stick to it because we feel passionate about a situation. Other times, we ignore a controversial stance because we really want to ride a certain attraction. Are we terrible people? Yep, sometimes we are. It's not always easy being a theme park fan because it's not always easy to be human.

Dreamlly's Theme Park Recommendation

SeaWorld
Orlando, Florida

After you've read the information and discussed it with your party, you may decide to visit a SeaWorld park. There is no judgment from me either way, and you can skip this section of the book if you decide that SeaWorld does not fit into your worldview. (But I'm not refunding any of your money because I already spent it on a jar of Dollywood apple butter.)

I prefer the SeaWorld in Orlando over its sisters in San Diego and San Antonio. The park in Orlando is larger, with more attractions. Also, Orlando provides roofs over the show arenas, and in San Diego, the guests have to sit in the sun. SeaWorld Orlando is the closest theme park to Orlando International Airport. It doesn't include any of its own hotels, but there is no lack of accommodations in this tourist haven.

Some people are surprised to learn that there are thrill rides at SeaWorld—there is more than fish here. In fact, the tallest, fastest, and longest roller coaster in Orlando is SeaWorld's Mako. (Mako is a type of really fast shark.) Even if you are not visiting SeaWorld, it's easy to spot Mako as you drive from the Orlando Airport toward Walt Disney World or Universal Studios. Kraken is Orlando's only floorless coaster. Manta is a head-first inverted coaster that is known as one of the smoothest in the world.

SeaWorld has a whole collection of rides for kids. Happy Harbor offers family rides and play areas that are themed after various ocean creatures. Sky Tower, a fixture at SeaWorld since it opened in 1974, is a four-hundred-foot observation tower—it's not a drop tower. Sky Tower is a nice, relaxing way to see much of central Florida.

Infinity Falls is SeaWorld's river raft ride. Built after the controversy of *Blackfish*, Infinity Falls has a strong message about taking care of Earth's rivers. But be advised, while learning about river conservation, you will get soaked. Absolutely-every-square-inch-soaked! The other major water ride, Journey to Atlantis, is a flume type ride that's themed after the famous lost civilization. Make sure to visit the gift shop at this ride's exit because there are some unique aquariums inside. (You can easily view the aquariums without going on the ride, if you like.)

Of course, SeaWorld has a lot of aquatic-related animals. Antarctica: Empire of the Penguin is one of the best penguin habitats in existence. After guests take a short ride on a trackless system, they enter the observation area to learn all about penguins. The ride is actually an innovative way of controlling the number of people who can be in the observation area. You will be able to see penguins both in and out of water. Just remember that penguins like it cold, and this is their home—not yours. It is quite cold inside the penguin habitat.

My favorite area in the park is Wild Arctic. After taking a simulated helicopter ride, you'll be able to explore the animals of the Arctic at your own pace. I love beluga whales because they always look so happy. (And belugas are the closest relatives to my cherished narwhals!) There are also seals and enormous walruses to view here.

TurtleTrek is a 3-D journey through the life of a giant sea turtle. Shark Encounter is a trip through one of the world's longest underwater tunnels. You will see sharks galore. Other viewing areas allow you to see manatees, manta rays, pelicans, and lots of other smaller animals.

The real stars of SeaWorld are the dolphins and the killer whales. There are underwater viewing opportunities for both of these animals. Just note that the killer whale viewing areas can, and do, change often as SeaWorld prepares to expand their habitat. If you're lucky, you may be able to see several baby dolphins at SeaWorld's dolphin nursery.

All of these attractions and animal exhibits are great and quite informative. But for me, the real reason to visit SeaWorld is to experience the wonder and awe of their shows. As someone who grew up as far away from an ocean as is possible in the US, the shows of SeaWorld were how I learned to appreciate and respect the amazing life of the seas. *One Ocean* is SeaWorld's main show that highlights the beauty and majesty of the killer whale. Yes, some people are there just to get splashed by the whales. But you'll see plenty of others who are there to appreciate these incredible animals. This is the show that inspired me to literally clean up my act. It's a bit strange to describe, but I somehow feel a personal connection to the whales as I watch them—I suspect this happens to many people. I'm inspired to make better choices about my interaction with the planet.

The dolphin show at SeaWorld is called *Dolphin Days.* There are also tropical birds in this show. The whole thing is choreographed to music and is as educational as it is entertaining. While not as inspiring as *One Ocean,* this show will also remind guests about the responsibility we all have to care for the oceans.

Clyde and Seamore's Sea Lion High is all entertainment. Sea lions, seals, and other critters present all sort of goofy antics. Usually I'm not a fan of this type of humor, but for some reason, this particular show just cracks me up.

Directly next to SeaWorld Orlando are two smaller parks. Discovery Cove is an interactive park that enables visitors to swim with dolphins. There are other exclusive activities at Discovery Cove, all made possible because this small park only allows a limited number of guests each day. A one-day ticket to Discovery Cove with a thirty-minute dolphin swim is $230.

Aquatica is SeaWorld's large water park. You can purchase all sorts of ticket packages to SeaWorld and Aquatica. Some of these packages include food.

Time will tell whether SeaWorld can weather the storm of

controversy. There is no doubt that many changes will occur at this park in the very near future. However, regardless of whether you visit SeaWorld or not, use the message of this park to inspire you to be a better Earthling.

Reason #18:

Positive bonding with family and friends at a theme park is in no way virtual.

An event occurred during the summer of 1996 that will forever be etched in my mind. Even though I've tried hard to forget it, I'm afraid it's one of those memories that will never die—memories experienced by a whole family are often like that.

I had just graduated from college and I joined my sister, Mom, Dad, Grandma, and Grandpa on a journey to our beloved Dollywood in Pigeon Forge, Tennessee. Back then, it was about a seventeen-hour drive. (We can make it in fifteen now.) We usually spent one night on the road and then continued toward Dolly Parton's magical paradise the next day. So on the second day, after about six hours of driving, we arrived at Dollywood's parking lot.

Those of you unfamiliar with Dollywood will need a little more information. The parking lot of this theme park is practically an attraction in itself. There isn't enough room for a sprawling span of asphalt; instead, the Dollywood lot is narrow and snakes around the base of a few Smoky Mountain foothills. It can be quite a walk, and Dollywood provides parking lot trams.

Mom, Dad, Grandma, and Grandpa got out of the van and started walking toward the tram. My sister and I wanted some exercise, and we began the long trek to the Dollywood entrance—we had gotten only about two hundred feet down the parking lot when a terrible noise stopped us in our tracks. Both my sister and I were startled by a horrible choking sound. I grabbed my sister's arm because I thought, for sure, that Grandpa was having a heart attack. The choking was accompanied by the wheezing sound of someone fighting for air. My own heart began to race.

I turned around and saw my parents running toward me. I got quite concerned. But then I noticed that my grandparents were walking to the tram stop. The horrible dying sound was coming from another guest, a man who was near my grandparents. This man was clearly in distress as he doubled over against the hood of a car. His whole body was shaking. Someone needed to help him, yet my grandparents seemed content to walk away.

"What the hell?" my sister exclaimed.

I was about to run over to the helpless man when my parents caught up to us. My mom grabbed my arm and pushed us all forward.

"Just keep walking," she said in an urgent voice.

"What's going on?" I asked as the four of us quickly moved through the cars.

"Just keep walking," Mom said again urgently.

"Jesus Ch—," my dad said. (Only he said the whole word.) "Grandma started walking and let fly with the loudest fart I've ever heard in my life."

It took me a moment to realize what he had said.

"Then what's wrong with that man?" asked my sister.

Dad answered, "Grandma didn't know he was there—he was right behind her. He's laughing so hard that he can't even walk."

Relieved that nobody was dying, I asked, "Why aren't you going on the tram?"

Dad replied, "I'm not going to be stuck on a tram with a farting old woman. It's embarrassing enough already."

To this day, Grandma still defends herself by blaming the long car ride. She is now ninety-eight, and over twenty years later, we continue to bring up this story from time to time. Sometimes my sister and I laugh so hysterically about it that we also start wheezing.

There are theme park critics out there who despise my obsession. They think theme parks are fake and shallow. Some critics of theme parks question the sanity of those of us who like to hang out in virtual worlds. I would like to assure these critics: There was nothing virtual about my grandma's fart.

The whole point of hanging out with family and friends is to make memories that strengthen the relationships. It doesn't matter if the memories were created in a theme park, a national park, or even in your own living room. I'm merely asking the critics to acknowledge that theme parks are about a whole lot more than just making money.

I sometimes wonder about the laughing man who was doubled over in the Dollywood parking lot. First, I hope he survived. Second, I hope he has enjoyed this memory over the years as much as we have. It would be wonderful if somewhere there is a man saying to his grandkids, "Honest to God, kids, it really did happen. I'm not joking—I really heard the loudest fart in my life from an old woman in the Dollywood parking lot by tram stop C!"

Let the memories live on!

Dreamlly's Theme Park Recommendation

Disney Cruiseline
Various Oceans around the World

Yes, I'm stretching my definition of theme park on this one. Earlier, I stated that a theme park has to be in one permanent location so that it could provide a sense of home. Even though the ships of Disney Cruiseline move around, their physical construction remains the same. The ships definitely provide a sense of home to me, and that's why I've decided to highlight these floating theme parks.

Discard any previous feelings you have about the cruise industry. Disney does it differently. There are no casinos. No smoking. No drunk spring-breakers. No nickel-and-diming around every corner. The Disney ships are spectacularly clean.

Currently, Disney Cruiseline contains four ships in its fleet. Disney Magic and Disney Wonder are the first, and a bit smaller, ships. Disney Dream and Disney Fantasy, the bigger sisters, are newer. However, Disney Cruiseline has three new ships on order and will start sailing them in 2020.

The Disney Dream and Disney Fantasy never leave the Caribbean. The Disney Dream provides three- and four-night cruises to complete a Walt Disney World vacation. The Disney Fantasy cruises on seven-night itineraries deeper into the Caribbean.

The Disney Magic spends its winter in the Caribbean. Toward May, this ship sails up the east coast to spend some time in New York City before crossing the Atlantic. The Disney Magic sails throughout Europe all summer, returning to Florida via New York City in the fall. Likewise, the Disney Wonder spends all winter in the Caribbean. In May, this ship crosses through the Panama Canal and heads up the west coast to Vancouver. From here, the Disney Wonder presents Alaskan cruises all summer. In the fall, the Disney Wonder returns to Florida though the Panama Canal.

Regardless of which ship and itinerary you choose, you'll be treated to the cream of the crop of Disney entertainment. Taking a Disney cruise is sort of like being at Disneyland for multiple days, but if they only let 2,500 other people in with you. Virtually all of the theme park principles that I acknowledge in this book are present on each of the Disney ships.

If you decide to take a journey to the Caribbean (including the Bahamas), you'll be treated to a day at Disney's private island Castaway Cay. This is perhaps the most serene place on Earth. The large family beaches of fine sand are perfect for enjoying the pristine water. Snorkeling is one of the main activities on Castaway Cay because Donald Duck has hidden all sorts of special items in the water to view. You'll find sunken ships, treasure, and amazing statues. (When Donald was hiding all this stuff, he was wearing a swimming suit. Then, why doesn't he wear pants on land? The world may never know.)

There are lots of other activities for children on Castaway Cay, including an interactive water play area. Teens and pre-teens each have their own island hangouts as well. And adults will find Serenity Bay, an adults-only beach far away from the family activities. Castaway Cay has its own dining facilities and shops. There's a lot to explore here—including trails for biking and just strolling around. When I think of paradise, I think of Castaway Cay.

If Castaway Cay was the only fun experience of a Disney Cruise, they would still be great. But there is so much more! The ships are full of activities. Each age group of kids has their own club where they can hang out, party, take a class, and generally just be kids. All of these activities are included in the price of your cruise. I've never seen out-of-control kids on a Disney Cruise because the kids are way too occupied. Each time I've sailed with kids, they have been sound asleep by 10:00 p.m. due to all the activity.

Food is an essential part of a Disney Cruise. Each ship contains three elaborately themed restaurants that passengers and their waiters rotate through. In addition to the restaurants, there is a buffet and room service. Unlike all other cruise lines, soft drinks are complimentary on a Disney ship, as is room service.

There isn't any smoky casino on any of Mickey's boats. Instead, adults can enjoy an entertainment district with various venues. Each ship has a sports bar, dance club, martini room, and wine bar.

The shows on Disney Cruiseline are second to none. These are Broadway-caliber extravaganzas that feature outstanding sets with amazing costumes. Expect great singing, excellent dancing, and unbelievable storytelling at each show. Remember, Disney has decades of experience when it comes to live entertainment, and you won't be disappointed.

Your destination will determine what type of experiences you have while on shore. In each port, passengers can choose from a wealth of Disney excursions. There's always a city tour offered at each stop, accompanied by very active to quite passive excursions. Of course, you're always free to go off on your own.

Just like in the theme parks, Disney Cruiseline celebrates Halloween and Christmas with themed cruises. Due to the time-line, most of these will be Caribbean or Bahaman cruises. Yes, there is trick-or-treating during Halloween. Yes, there is a gigantic Christmas tree in the atrium during Christmas. And yes, it does snow on Castaway Cay for the holidays! (It's Disney snow, but magical nonetheless.)

The amazing family bonding moments on one of these jour-neys come from all the Disney touches. You'll be able to meet lots of Disney characters without waiting in much of a line. You may exit the elevator and literally run into Minnie Mouse or Cinderella. Once, my sister didn't realize that Captain Hook was sneaking up right behind her. When she heard a sound, she quickly turned and saw his enormous head in front of her face. She screamed so loud that security ran over. Now, this is a bonding moment none of us will ever forget.

Reason #19:

Facing fear inside a theme park prepares people to face it outside the park.

Earlier in this book, I talked about developing the art of patience though practice. I believe the same is true about fear.

Think back to your first day at a new school. For some of you, that day literally may have been yesterday. For others of us, that day was considerably further in the past. Regardless, do you remember how you felt on that day? More than likely, you were full of all kinds of fear. You worried about whether you'd find your way. You worried about your classes and teachers. You worried about lunch and if you'd find someone to sit with. On that day, fear was close to you. But the second day was easier. By the time Christmas came around, your new school was just as familiar as your home. You triumphed over the fear of joining a new culture.

As life moves forward, the experience of attending a new school is repeated. (Sorry to break the news to any young readers out there, but fear doesn't end in high school.) Throughout life, we attend many new schools and conquer a lot of cafeterias. There are first days at new jobs, first days in new cities, and first dinners with future in-laws.

Despite what the pessimists out there want to believe, fear does get easier. Each new experience is slightly more manageable. This is because our brains have built synapses that lead us through the fear. Just as exercise strengthens muscles, each new fear strengthens our brain's synapses.

Let's pause to listen to the words of the great Eleanor Roosevelt. Here is a woman who experienced fear. It can't have been easy to wake up every morning knowing that your husband was leading a nation which might, at any moment, be attacked on either coast. Eleanor says, "You gain strength, courage, and confidence by every experience in which you really stop to look fear in the face. You are able to say to yourself, 'I lived through this horror. I can take the next thing that comes along.'"

For me, the word in Mrs. Roosevelt's quote that resonates the most with me is *confidence*. It's not that I've obliterated fear, but I know I can face it because I have before. Confidence isn't just believing in yourself—it's *knowing* in yourself.

I love seeing the face of a kid who's just exited a roller coaster for the first time. It's a look of total triumph. In this moment, the kid knows that she or he can face anything. Of course, this feeling of invincibility wanes when another, higher coaster presents itself. But in time, new synapses are formed with each more terrifying coaster.

However, there is another moment of the roller coaster experience that is much more important than the triumphal exit. There is a ritual that goes along with boarding a coaster. While you are waiting in line, doubts start to form—the brain questions whether this act can be accomplished. With each step closer to the front of the line, the body responds with a faster heart rate and increased adrenaline. But just as it seems impossible, a patterned process of physical action begins. The body sits in a seat.

Harnesses are buckled and snapped into place. The coaster attendants perform their checks and double checks. All these physical processes keep the body at ease. Then, there is the inevitable point of no return. There is no backing out as the train begins to move. There is a brief moment of panic that is quelled by trust.

Some of you may be thinking, "Good Lord! It's just a roller coaster—it's not like you've faced an inferno, or a tsunami, or something catastrophic." Well, you're right. I don't know what it's like to face a tsunami. But I do know what it's like to face a horrible boss, a near miss on the highway, and a severe thunderstorm. It's these types of daily fears that theme parks prepare us for. When I'm in these situations, I tell myself to remember the ritual: The triumph over a questioning mind by relying on physical sensations and a bit of trust.

Dreamlly's Theme Park Recommendation

Cedar Point
Sandusky, Ohio

Cedar Point is the self-proclaimed "Roller Coaster Capital of the World"—and it probably is. This park doesn't have the most coasters; however, it unarguably has the most impressive collection of coasters on the planet. In fact, Cedar Point contains 60,423 feet of roller coaster track. That's 11.4 miles—it's the most of any park in the world. Six coasters at Cedar Point have a drop that is over two hundred feet. No other park can claim that. Five of Cedar Point's coasters have a drop of ninety degrees or more. No other park can claim that, either.

A *hypercoaster* is any roller coaster with a height taller than two hundred feet. The first hypercoaster in existence was Magnum XL-200 at Cedar Point. (Its first drop is 205 feet.) *Gigacoaster* is the term for a roller coaster that's taller than three hundred feet. Cedar Point's Millennium Force was the world's first gigacoaster with its 310-foot peak. Of course, it doesn't end there. The first *stratacoaster* on the planet was Cedar Point's Top Thrill Dragster, with a height of 420 feet. (You guessed it—a stratacoaster must have at least a four-hundred-foot drop.) Top Thrill Dragster reaches speeds of 120 miles per hour. There isn't currently a word for coasters in excess of 499 feet. (In some crazy designer's mind, there is a five-hundred-foot coaster—that person deserves to be able to create a label for it.)

Cedar Point's Steel Vengeance is the world's first hybrid hypercoaster. A hybrid coaster uses a steel track on a wood frame. Since Steel Vengeance uses this type of track and offers a 205-foot drop, it's a hybrid hypercoaster. This coaster also gives riders twenty-nine seconds of airtime—the most of any coaster anywhere. (Airtime occurs when the inertia of the coaster allows the riders' bodies to oppose gravity.) In addition, Steel Vengeance has four inversions because, at Cedar Point, hyper-height and zero gravity just isn't enough.

As you see, Cedar Point is definitely a place where guests need to conquer their fear. However, if you're not able to attempt the hyper, hybrid, giga, or strata, there are fourteen other coasters to try. Each of these remaining coasters would make any other park jealous, but at Cedar Point, they just become the "also rans"—that's how unbelievably crazy this park has become!

The fun doesn't stop with coasters. Cedar Point holds a

240-foot drop tower and one of the tallest extreme swings in the world. There are also attractions that can't really be described: MaxAir is this sort of pendulum turning swing machine that holds riders upside down at 140 feet. I don't know who thinks of these things, but they owe me $12.76 for the lunch that I lost.

Technically, Cedar Point has embraced more of an iron park philosophy in the recent years. There is some theming in the Frontiertown section, but the rest of the park is divided into several different midways. Planet Snoopy, the children's area, has a bit of a Peanuts theme—but nothing like Camp Snoopy at Knott's Berry Farm.

Cedar Point has a very long history that can be traced back to the nineteenth century. The park is located on a small island that juts out into Lake Erie (there is a causeway that makes driving easy). Originally owned by a railroad company, Cedar Point is a classic end-of-the-line park that was built to encourage passengers to ride the weekend trains. The location is stunning. Cedar Point provides a bit of the classic ocean-front beach vibe to the people of the landlocked American Midwest.

Located in Sandusky, Ohio, Cedar Point is about sixty miles west of Cleveland and sixty miles east of Toledo. It's also a two-hour drive from both Columbus and Detroit. I live in a state that borders one of the Great Lakes, but I know that many of you on the coasts tend to see this part of the world as fly-over country. I encourage all of you to visit at least one of the Great Lakes—they are amazing with beautiful shores, their own microclimates, and all that serene water.

If you visit Cedar Point, you can stay in its marina, cabins, or campground, or in one of three hotels. The venerable Hotel Breakers dates from 1905. This hotel looks like it belongs on the coast of California. It's a full-service resort with pools, restaurants, and special access to the park.

In addition to all of this, Cedar Point has a water park called Cedar Point Shores. It's a world-class water park with all the attractions you'd expect to find. Also, Cedar Point takes advantage of its lakeside location. A pristine one-mile stretch of beach is available for anyone who has a theme park admission ticket. Guests of any of the Cedar Point Resorts and season pass holders are also welcome to use the beach. It's quite clean and was actually the park's first attraction! On the beach, guests can rent jet skis, speedboats, paddleboards, and kayaks. Fishing charters and parasailing are also available.

I love theme parks that have their own history museums on their property. Town Hall Museum, located in Cedar Point's Frontiertown, presents artifacts from the park's long history. It's great to see a park take pride in all the attractions and people that literally built their past. A special note to all the thrill-seekers out there: Sure, you've got a lot of coasters to ride here. And the thought of going to a boring museum may be scary. But please, face your fear and give it a shot—pay homage to those who believe that the world is more than just work.

Reason #20:

Some of the planet's most amazing architecture and landscaping is found inside theme parks.

An iconic ribbed cone with spires covers Space Mountain at the Disney Parks in California, Florida, Tokyo, Hong Kong, and Paris. (Paris's version is more colorful than the standard white found in the other parks.) These structures are instantly recognizable. Space Mountain is designed to invoke the fantasy of a futuristic building on a far-off planet. However, even though its function is fantasy, it still had to be designed in the real world.

I'm going to rely heavily on the Disney Parks in this section. Not because they alone hold the virtue of architecture, but mostly because the Disney Parks are older and better publicized—thus, their structures are more iconic and can be pictured instantly. Another case in point is Epcot's large geodesic dome called Spaceship Earth. This masterpiece of design and engineering evokes the massiveness of Earth while floating lightly on a pedestal. (Students of architecture will be quick to point out that Spaceship Earth is actually a geodesic sphere—somehow the label of geodesic dome stuck.)

The famous Disney castles are not original ideas. Walt Disney drew inspiration for his first castle from King Ludwig II of Bavaria's Neuschwanstein Castle in Germany. Still, someone had to design the Disney versions—and engineer them, build them, paint them, decorate them, etc. Behind every piece of theme park magic is an awful lot of work.

Mickey Mouse's newest home in Shanghai, open less than two years, is already home to some stunning architecture in its own right. Instead of Space Mountain, Shanghai has a coaster based on the TRON films. The enormous curving domes of TRON Lightcycle Power Run catch every guest's eye as he or she approaches the park. At night, the domes glow with beautiful and constantly changing lights. If you look close enough, you'll eventually see a flash of light trace the curve of the domes—this is actually the coaster itself as it gracefully propels passengers through the night.

The Tree of Life, the centerpiece of Disney's Animal Kingdom in Florida, isn't a tree at all. It's a building that holds a theater—someone had to design that too. Even though Japan is a country full of volcanos, Mount Prometheus at Tokyo DisneySea is not natural. It's a massive structure that was designed to hold two major attractions, a restaurant, a shop, a tunnel system, and even a small lake. Oh, it also erupts periodically. A faux-mountain is not the same type of architecture you'll find in most cities, but it's architecture nonetheless. Some very smart and creative people are behind this structure.

The Haunted Mansion at Disneyland in California looks like an antebellum plantation house because it's found in New Orleans Square. At Walt Disney World in Florida, the Haunted Mansion is an old Hudson River Valley estate because it's located in Liberty Square. A creepy neo-Victorian frontier house holds the

Haunted Mansion in Frontierland at Disneyland Paris. There isn't a Haunted Mansion at Hong Kong Disneyland. Instead, this park contains Mystic Manor. The colorful turrets of this strange structure beckon guests from across the park. It's part prairie-style house, part Russian church, and part Victorian mansion. But it all goes together seamlessly and looks like it belongs.

Speaking of Hong Kong Disneyland, so as not to offend the local population, Disney employed several masters of feng shui during the design phase of the park. These masters had a voice in the early stages and are responsible for Hong Kong Disneyland's harmonious orientation between mountains and the sea. Their work is simply stunning. You can almost see the good energy flowing into Mickey's realm as it pours down the mountains and up from the harbor.

Believe it or not, there are people who go to theme parks and never ever go on any ride or see any show. They are not there for the shops and food, either. These people come to literally stop and smell the roses. If it weren't for theme parks, there would be a lot of unemployed botanists running around.

If you take the Backstage Magic tour at Walt Disney World, you will get to visit Disney's enormous nursery. Here, dozens of designers create the thousands of hanging floral baskets that hang in the theme parks and resorts. Arborists and botanists are on hand to care for sick trees and plants. If any foliage does happen to die, a fully-grown replacement is quickly planted for the enjoyment of the next day's guests. Disney has entire greenhouses full of mums for the fall. There are many more greenhouses full of poinsettias ready for the holidays.

We can leave Mickey and friends for a moment to admire some other amazing theme park landscaping. Busch Gardens in both Tampa and Williamsburg do not take their name lightly.

Landscaped gardens are a fixture of these parks and, in both cases, are worth the price of admission. I've never seen more pumpkins in my life than when I visited Europa-Park one October. It was breathtaking. Some parks are in such gorgeous locations that they don't need a lot of professional help. A great example of this is Dollywood, where in the fall, the Smoky Mountains provide a spectacular backdrop of colors behind the roller coasters.

Theme parks don't just happen. They are planned by thousands of talented people. These people aren't just architects, botanists, engineers, and designers. They are also artists, and I thank them for living.

Dreamlly's Theme Park Recommendation

Disneyland Parc
Paris, France

Forget everything you've ever heard about EuroDisney. It's not a huge failure. It's not bankrupt. It's not even called EuroDisney anymore. There was a lot of bad press when this park opened in 1992, mostly because the press was just aching for it to be bad. Certainly, this property has had some struggles, but what theme park hasn't?

Disneyland Paris, renamed to better reflect its brand, includes two theme parks and several resort hotels. Disneyland Parc and Walt Disney Studios are easily walkable from each other. The entire resort is one twenty-minute train ride from central Paris. It's located in the beautiful rolling countryside of Marne-la-Vallée.

There is a reason why the architecture is so stunning at Disneyland Parc—it all comes down to pride and ego. Michael Eisner was the head of Disney during the development and design phase of this park. He and his team were promising to build an amazing European version of the famous park that had done so well in California, Florida, and Japan. However, the French press was not all that happy to see a piece of America being built so close to their beloved Paris.

Mr. Eisner and his Imagineers responded to the criticism by leaving nothing off the table. They would make this park so undeniably gorgeous that not even the most French of French critics would complain. Each of the resort's hotels was designed by a world-class architect. Famed architect Michael Graves designed Disney's Hotel New York. It's reminiscent of the New York skyline without being reminiscent of the New York skyline—it's brilliant.

La Chateau de la Belle au Bois Dormant, aka Sleeping Beauty Castle, is not like its fiberglass sisters around the world. This castle is built from real stone. It's the most unique of all the Disney castles with its pink hues and towering turrets. While I love seeing any Disney castle, at Disneyland Parc in Paris, I cannot keep my eyes off of it. It's a masterpiece of design.

On its second floor, elaborate stained-glass windows tell the story of Sleeping Beauty. But Mr. Eisner wasn't going to have just any artist make the glass. He wanted the best. Unfortunately, the best stained glass expert in the world was working on refurbishing the famous windows of Notre Dame Cathedral at the time. But that expert put the Archbishop of Paris on hold for a bit when Disney offered him more money.

All of this unprecedented building came with a price. That

price was more than what Michael Eisner actually had in his wallet, and thus began the negative press. But after some reorganization, rebranding, and hard work, Disneyland Paris is currently making money. (The park is now entirely owned by the Walt Disney Company. Mickey Mouse purchased all remaining shares in 2017, and Disneyland Paris Resort is no longer a public company on the French market.)

Yep, all this beautiful architecture is due to a good ego and a bad bookkeeper. But when I walk around the place, it really doesn't matter to me. I'm so appreciative of the quality that I'm glad it happened the way it did.

Of course, there is more than architecture to this park. Most of the classic Disney attractions are here, along with a few surprises. One of the things I love best about Disneyland Parc are the walk-through attractions. The other Disney parks don't have as many, and they aren't done as well. The walk-through to see the story of Sleeping Beauty and its amazing windows is inspirational. It's located inside the castle through a clearly marked stairway.

There is a walk-through in the fort that separates Frontierland from the rest of the park. Guests can explore the many rooms of the fort and see what the American pioneers are up to. In Adventureland, there is a walk-through that tells the story of Aladdin. There's never a line to see either of these attractions.

On the island right outside Pirates of the Caribbean, you can walk through a pirate ship and explore all kinds of themed caves. On a hot day, this is a perfect place to get out of the sun. The best walk-through in the park is in Discoveryland (Disneyland Parc's version of Tomorrowland). Here, you can tour the Nautilus submarine from *20,000 Leagues under the Sea*. This attraction is as detailed as it gets. Any fan of Jules Verne will want to put this walk-through on her or his list.

Lastly, walk through the small passage under the castle. Here in this cave, you'll encounter an amazing sight—an enormous dragon! The dragon is impressive, and you'll want to spend some time watching him. (I don't know if it's a he or she, but he looks quite angry at times, so I'll go with he. But, then again, the dragon might be pregnant. I guess I'm really not sure.) The dragon randomly sleeps, breathes, wakes up, blows fire around, and then sleeps again. Sometimes as it's sleeping, you'll see just these giant claws lightly tap the stone. Now, that's a creepy attention to detail!

Just promise me one thing: If you visit Disneyland Parc in Paris, make sure to give yourself plenty of time to do nothing. Don't spend your whole trip waiting in line to ride Pirates of the Caribbean. Don't waste an entire night in a restaurant or shop. At this park, you'll want to spend the majority of your time just plain walking around. Walk in the morning, afternoon, and night. Just like Monet, experience the park in all the different kinds of light. Look up, down, and all around at the amazing detail. Realize that this is what can happen when talented people are given the means to accomplish true beauty.

Reason #21:

Nostalgia is truly a magical experience; theme parks have plenty of it.

It's the music that gets me every time. We often forget that music has to be designed just as much as architecture. All theme parks present carefully chosen music to set the perfect mood for the guests. All parks have music around their entrance gates, but some even have it in the parking lot. There is no mistaking that you're at Dollywood when you hear the iconic trills of Dolly Parton's crystal voice soaring above the hills. The symphonic score of an adventure film signals that you are about to enter Universal's Islands of Adventure in Orlando. Parks in the Six Flags chain use recent hits to set the tone.

In Minneapolis, our annual Fourth of July fireworks are presented along the Mississippi riverfront. It's quite nice, as old flour mills frame the display and the weather is finally warm enough to be outside without a parka. But no matter how spectacular the display is, nobody in the audience cries. Now consider the fireworks at Disneyland. It's difficult to find dry eyes in that crowd. The difference is the music. During Disney's amazing displays, the music of your childhood is loudly broadcast all around you. If it's not the music of your childhood, then it's the music of your children's childhood or your parents' childhood.

It is impossible to describe the power of music. It comes from some primal place deep within us. The same can be said about nostalgia.

For me, nostalgia is a complicated emotion. It's the only emotion I can think of that is both happy and sad at the same time. I get emotional each time I hear "When You Wish upon a Star" during the fireworks at a Disney Park. I feel so happy to be there at that moment to experience the sights, sounds, and smells of Main Street, USA. But I'm also profoundly sad in a way that I can't describe. Then, oddly, I'm happy that I'm sad. Indeed, the whole thing is very Freudian.

The word *nostalgia* can be traced back to Europe in the seventeenth century. At that time, the feeling of nostalgia was considered a negative emotion to experience. In fact, the word comes from the Greek *nostos*, which means "a homeward journey," and the Greek *algos*, which means "sorrow." Nostalgia can still be considered a mental illness today for the person who dwells upon it too long and develops a depression.

I'm not, by any means, someone who craves the "good old days." On the contrary, I don't think there ever were old days full of good things. Seriously, how could anyone have had a good day before there was electricity? What did they possibly do? Not to mention that for much of the good old days, women were property, minorities had to sit in the back of the bus, and gay people were killed. Nope, I don't yearn to go back in time. But I still feel nostalgia.

I read a research paper about nostalgia written by Dr. Clay Routledge, a psychologist who studied the emotion in American and Dutch college students. He asked the students to read a series of news articles about horrible events. After reading, the students used a scale to rate their reaction to each piece of news. However, half the students were told to wait in another room while the other half took the exam. While the waiting students were waiting, popular music from their high school years was played throughout the room. In the end, the students who had been exposed to nostalgic music felt overwhelmingly more positive about their future—even after reading horrible news articles. Dr. Routledge writes, "Nostalgia serves a crucial existential function. It brings to mind cherished experiences that assure us we are valued people who have meaningful lives. Some of our research shows that people who regularly engage in nostalgia are better at coping with concerns about death."

It makes me feel better to know that I'm not alone in my complicated relationship with nostalgia. When I visit a theme park, it's not that I wish the park was just like it was in 1976. It's not that I want to go back in time, and it's not that I'm missing some of the people who aren't with me. I don't want the good old days. However, I am yearning for something—but something that I can't quite name.

I imagine myself cooking with a big pot that's hanging over a raging fire. Into the pot I throw these English words: *home, innocence, regret, love, winter,* and *peace.* Those six words melt in the pot, and I stir them together. The resulting soup is nostalgia. I can't decide if I like the soup or not, but the experience of making it has made me feel so very human.

Dreamlly's Theme Park Recommendation

Disneyland
Anaheim, California

Disneyland, the happiest place on earth, oozes nostalgia around every corner. Sure, some of it comes from Walt Disney himself. He sketched the park on a napkin, had a hand in designing its iconic appearance, and broadcast the park into the American living room. But the nostalgia mostly comes from the millions of visitors, many of them local, who call Disneyland their home park.

The Disneyland Resort is in Anaheim, California. Depending upon the time of your journey, it can be quite easy or excruciatingly difficult to reach. The legendary Los Angeles traffic is as bad as it's depicted on television—but the highways are wide, with many lanes. I've found that approaching Anaheim is fairly easy. However, driving the few blocks from the freeway to the resort can take quite a while. Give yourself plenty of time.

There are two theme parks here: the original Disneyland and its cousin, Disney California Adventure. (Okay, Disney California Adventure isn't really a first cousin—it's more like a fourth cousin twice removed.) There are some excellent attractions and a fantastic evening show at Disney California Adventure, but you'll want to spend most of your time at Disneyland.

The biggest difference between Disneyland and all the other

Disney Parks around the globe is the prevalence of the outside world. When the park was constructed in 1954, Walt didn't have the money to purchase large tracts of land. Disney, as a company, didn't have near the power it has today. Consequently, the outside world is right there on the other side of the gates. In fact, there are many places within the park where you can see non-Disney hotels and restaurants along Harbor Boulevard.

All of this adds to the nostalgic charm of Disneyland. Sure, there are a lot of kitschy places as you approach the resort. Some of Anaheim is downright crappy. But in a way, it makes the secluded magic of Disney that much more special.

This is Mickey, Minnie, Donald, Goofy, Daisy, and Pluto's first real home. To visit Mickey at Disneyland is to visit Mickey in the same place where Walt Disney visited Mickey. When you ride the Disneyland Railroad, you're riding on the very tracks where Walt Disney, Art Linkletter, and Ronald Reagan opened the park on July 15, 1955. (You've probably not heard of him, but Ronald Reagan was this minor actor and television personality. He emceed part of the live television coverage for the Disneyland's first day.)

While Florida has retired some vintage attractions, Disneyland, to its massive credit, has kept several of its original dark rides. You can still enjoy Mr. Toad's Wild Ride. (And then you can call me and explain the last scene because I just don't get it.) You can also ride Snow White's Scary Adventure, or as I like to call it, Snow White's Absolutely Terrifying Adventure.

Disneyland still contains a Pinocchio dark ride, a Winnie the Pooh attraction, and the first version of Peter Pan's Flight. It's the only park with a dark ride based on *Alice in Wonderland*. Storybookland Canal Boats, a delightful journey through miniature vignettes of Disney films, has also been entertaining guests since the park's early days.

For roller coaster enthusiasts, Disneyland doesn't have any of the tallest or fastest. But it does have a coaster with great historical appeal. The Matterhorn was the very first steel coaster in the world. It's still in operation today inside a replica of the Swiss mountain. The Matterhorn was the first of Disney's faux mountains, and its innovative engineering is the basis for all theme park mountains to this day.

Though the route has changed a bit over of the years, the iconic Disneyland Monorail continues to transport guests from Tomorrowland to the Disneyland Hotel. The first family to take a ride on the monorail was Mr. and Mrs. Richard Nixon and their daughters. (He was vice president at the time.) Literally, kings and queen have ridden the monorail. When dignitaries visit California, Disneyland remains at the top of their list of things they want to see.

Back in Main Street, USA, history buffs will not want to miss Great Moments with Mr. Lincoln. This is the original show from the 1964-65 World's Fair in New. York. It's as awe inspiring today as it was back then. Lincoln can stand, gesture, talk, and sit all on his own. Remember, in 1964, nobody had ever seen anything like this. Reportedly, the sight of Lincoln talking and moving was so shocking that many people fainted at the sight.

Other attractions imported to Disneyland from the New York World's Fair include portions of the dioramas inside the tunnel of the Disneyland Railroad. At the World's Fair, Pepsi hired Walt to create an attraction that could also raise money for UNICEF. Walt and designer Mary Blair created the ultimate in nostalgia, "it's a small world." It's been copied several times at other Disney

Parks, but the original, direct from the World's Fair, is here in Disneyland.

To view the quintessential act of nostalgia, just stand in Town Square at the end of Main Street, USA. Look for the fire station next to the town hall. The station, like everything else around you, is as charming as can be. You'll notice that there's a lamp burning in the upstairs window. This was Walt's private apartment inside the park. Because Anaheim is a bit of a distance from the Disney Studios in Burbank, Walt often slept at Disneyland. Each morning, the cast members of the park would arrive at work and look for the lamp. If the lamp was lit, it meant that Walt was on the premises.

After Walt's untimely death in 1966, someone had the idea that the lamp should never be turned off. This was a way to remember that Walt Disney was, and is, always at Disneyland. Over the years, the lamp was only turned off when Mrs. Lillian Disney or one of her two daughters visited the park. Since all three have now gone on to stay with Walt at that big Disneyland in the sky, the lamp has never been extinguished.

Reason #22:

Theme parks aren't isolated, as they exist in real communities with physical infrastructure.

Most people in the western hemisphere think of Hong Kong as a large, cosmopolitan city. It certainly is. But most of us don't realize that Hong Kong is really a collection of 261 islands and one peninsula. Hong Kong Island isn't even the largest island in the group. The most densely populated district in Hong Kong is Kowloon. Kowloon isn't on an island and is part of the peninsula connected to mainland China. Somewhere among all of this is Ocean Park.

Ocean Park would have to close its gates today if people couldn't access it. It's located on the edge of Hong Kong Island, but many of the employees live in Kowloon, Lantau Island, or one of the other 259 islands. Of course, lots of Ocean Park's visitors come from the local area. But there are also many visitors from mainland China, Japan, the US, and other places all around the globe. None of this could happen if Ocean Park did not play well with others.

For someone like me, infrastructure can be fascinating and

fun. Trains, tunnels, bridges, ferries, airports, freeways, subways, Shinkansen—I love all this stuff. Unfortunately for the civic planners and taxpayers, infrastructure is just so darn expensive.

Tsing Ma Bridge connects Kowloon and Hong Kong's largest island of Lantau. Lantau Island is home to both Hong Kong Disneyland and Hong Kong International Airport. The bridge holds six lanes of traffic on its upper deck. The lower deck handles trains and includes ingenious coverable traffic lanes for use during typhoons. It cost just under one billion in US dollars to build, and nearly a hundred thousand cars cross the bridge each day.

Interstate 4 in Orlando connects the world's busiest theme park resort to—well—the next of the world's busiest theme park resorts. I don't think the highways of central Florida have stopped construction since the Magic Kingdom opened in 1971. (Unfortunately, that's not a joke.)

If you build it, they will come. They're just not going to apparate out of thin air, however, like they do in the Harry Potter books. They are going to come by planes, cars, trains, boats, and the power of their own feet. It's up to the communities surrounding a park to provide these things.

The big names like Disney and Universal are able to wield considerable power with local city councils. They receive large tax breaks. But to be fair, they return the community with lots of jobs and the money from all the visitors who stay in hotels and eat at restaurants. It's a bit challenging, however, for small local parks to gain the same advantage.

In some rare cases, theme parks get lucky and get to use existing infrastructure. In 1982, the Hubert H. Humphrey Metrodome opened in downtown Minneapolis. Until that time, the Minnesota Twins and Minnesota Vikings played in a stadium directly across a major freeway from the Minneapolis-St. Paul International Airport. When the sports teams left, they vacated a prime piece of real estate. At that time, MSP Airport had developed into Northwest Airlines' hub for Asian and European flights. Before being purchased by Delta Airlines, Northwest was one of the largest in the world. Consequently, the MSP Airport is one of the busiest layover airports on the planet.

A large piece of vacant property next to hundreds of hotels, several major freeways, and a busy airport doesn't become available very often. This was a case of the infrastructure waiting for an attraction. In 1992, the Mall of America opened on this spot, complete with the country's largest indoor theme park, Knott's Camp Snoopy. Today, the mall has expanded its footprint several times, and Knott's Camp Snoopy is now Nickelodeon Universe.

None of this was easy. I was in high school during this time, and the controversy was fierce. It took a lot of people to accomplish a lot of hard work in order for the Mall of America to happen. Was it worth it? The thirteen thousand people who work at the mall probably think it was. As do the people who benefit from the forty-two million annual visitors.

Infrastructure can, unfortunately, place increased stress on the physical environment surrounding it. However, theme parks have been on the forefront of taking action to care for the planet. Long before "green" became a label for environmentally friendly policies, Walt Disney World in Florida implemented a recycling and energy-reduction project. In fact, the Magic Kingdom started sorting its trash on the first day it opened in 1971. Today, Walt Disney World produces its own electricity, much of it from solar panels, and operates one of the largest recycling centers in the United States.

You won't find any recycling bins at Dollywood—and that's,

ironically, very good for the environment. Years ago, Dollywood became a founding member of an organization dedicated to preserving the beauty of the Smoky Mountains. This effort eventually turned into a massive facility that sorts all the waste of Sevier County, the county where Dollywood is located. Using humans and technology, the trash is sorted during a three-mile long conveyer process. Everything is stripped to its smallest components and either recycled, resold, or turned into black dirt inside their huge composting facility. No resident or business recycles in Sevier County, yet this county recycles more weight per capita than any other county in the entire nation. A portion of every Dollywood ticket goes to this amazing project that is now studied and copied all around the globe.

Whether it's building roads or taking care of waste, people have to work together to make theme parks a reality. That reality requires a lot of people working with many different organizations. A bridge just isn't a physical structure—it's also a symbol of the ability for people to work together. It gives me hope for the future that we, as a species, can still make these things happen. In a world as divisive as ours, it brings me joy that Dollywood, Silver Dollar City, Valleyfair, and countless other parks have the community support they need to operate. We must work together in order to play together.

Dreamlly's Theme Park Recommendation

Ocean Park
Hong Kong SAR, China

Ocean Park has it all. It's part Six Flags, part SeaWorld, and part San Diego Zoo. The park has these adorable mascots you can have your photo taken with, so perhaps it's part Disney too. And, Ocean Park has pandas! You can't go all the way to China and not see a panda!

In a city of complex public transportation, it's not hard to get to Ocean Park. Just make your way to the Admiralty station in central Hong Kong. You can get there via metro, bus, or Star Ferry. If you're on the Kowloon side, take the Star Ferry. It costs literally 15 cents (US) and provides the best boat tour of any city anywhere. At Admiralty station, look for the South Island Line of the MTR metro. Take the South Island Line due south.

Ocean Park is across Hong Kong Island from Victoria Harbor. It's a part of the island that most tourists never visit. But you're not most tourists because you've been reading this book. The metro ride across the island is quite unique, as you'll pass through densely populated neighborhoods and rolling jungle hills. Ocean Park has its own stop. (Also, for an added touch of engineering, the trains on the South Island Line are driverless!)

Ocean Park provides a great example of the positive benefits of competition. Many people predicted that Ocean Park would close soon after Hong Kong Disneyland opened in 2005. However, all the international visitors to Hong Kong Disneyland wanted other things to do, and Ocean Park actually increased its attendance. Park officials quickly got in gear and began a massive expansion project. Today, Ocean Park annually attracts 7.6 million visitors and is the thirteenth-most-visited theme park in the world.

Finding land where it was available, Ocean Park is actually divided by a large mountain into two different areas. You'll enter the park in the Waterfront area. To get to the Summit area, you'll need to choose either the cable car or the funicular. The cable car is one mile long and takes eight-minutes. It's simply spectacular, with incredible views of the South China Sea. The funicular takes only three-minutes and doesn't offer a view. It does, however, use screens to simulate the feeling that passengers are traveling through the sea.

All of the thrill rides are in the Summit area. There are four coasters, a drop tower, a log flume, and a river raft ride. Ocean Park has lots of smaller rides, and you could occupy an entire day just riding around the Summit. But you shouldn't. The animal exhibits here are top-notch.

The polar-themed area of the Summit is amazing, with hundreds of penguins. (There is a penguin-themed restaurant that offers fantastic views while you dine.) The polar area also includes sea lions, walruses, and snow-white owls. The arctic fox den is one of my favorite spots in the park. Another favorite spot is nearby Sea Jelly Spectacular. Although this attraction could just as well be called Aliens Floating in Tanks: There are thousands of jellyfish on display in large cylinder tanks that you can walk around. It's educational, creepy, and kind of beautiful.

Guests can see all types of tropical species in the rainforest section of the Summit. Many of these animals I had never heard of before.

After you've experienced the Summit, head back down to the Waterfront. You can use the same form of transportation or choose the other option. The Waterfront contains the Grand Aquarium—one of the largest in the world. Here, you can see over four hundred species of fish and aquatic mammals. Make sure to see the Panoramic Ocean Gallery. This space contains the world's largest aquarium viewing dome.

The other big star of the Waterfront is Amazing Asian Animals. This attraction is a star because it contains the one animal that everyone came to see: giant panda. I'm not sure exactly how many pandas live at Ocean Park. It's different each time I visit. But, rest assured, you will see multiple pandas doing all the things that pandas do—which is pretty much absolutely nothing. They are, however, just so darn adorable! Seriously, if you've never seen one, pandas are the only wild animal I've ever seen that I really want to hug. They'd probably rip my head off. Oh, well—it might be worth it.

There are lots of other Asian animals in this area. Because I grew up in the western hemisphere and my Asian education stopped at sweet and sour chicken, most of these animals are new to me. You'll find many types of monkeys, reptiles, and fish. All of the entire Asian section features lovely gardens of indigenous flowers.

A children's play area and a place to meet the cute mascots sits next to a location called Old Hong Kong. This is sort of like Main Street, USA, except that it's a street in—well—old Hong Kong. It's perfectly themed, and you can even ride in a rickshaw.

As you can see, there is a lot to do at Ocean Park. Just be advised: The humidity in the summer is intense. The same warning I posted for Hong Kong Disneyland applies here. When you are finished, it's an easy metro ride back to central Hong Kong, where you can make your way to an air-conditioned hotel.

Reason #23:

Theme parks provide economic resources with employment for millions.

The Industrial Revolution was not all it was cracked up to be. Work has hard in those days. In 1800, it was virtually unheard of for kids to hold actual jobs. But by 1900, 1.7 million children under the age of sixteen were working in the United States. The conditions were deplorable and wages extremely low. Many people were injured or killed while at work.

Work improved greatly in the twentieth century. However, it took two world wars and countless social movements to get us there. By the 1980s, it was much less likely that you'd be injured at work. But just as people were getting used to the spoils of industrialization, technology changed the world again. In the 1990s, the Industrial Revolution was left in the past—along with lots of jobs.

The Information Age brought with it a rise in travel and leisure. In 2016, we humans globally spent 8.27 trillion US dollars on travel and tourism. More than seventy-five million international visitors enter the United States each year. New York City and Orlando compete annually for the coveted prize of most-visited

US destination for international tourists. In recent years, Orlando has narrowly beaten New York City.

With the loss of factory and manufacturing jobs, the economies of most countries in the western hemisphere need travel and tourism. After air travel and accommodations, theme parks rank third in the amount of revenue produced for the travel industry.

Disneyland employs 23,000 people from the greater Los Angeles area. Six Flags employs 46,000 at its twenty properties in North America—most of them from large urban areas. Near Cleveland, Ohio, Cedar Point counts 5,800 employees. These statistics represent a lot of jobs. However, in large urban areas, there would be other jobs if the theme parks decided to cut back.

I'm more impressed with the number of jobs that theme parks provide in smaller markets. Dollywood employs 4,000 people in rural eastern Tennessee. Without Dollywood, these people would have few employment options to explore. Its sister park, Silver Dollar City, employs 2,000 people in equally rural southern Missouri. Knoebels Amusement Resort is located in Elysburg, Pennsylvania. The city of Elysburg has 2,194 residents. Without Knoebels, the largest theme park in the United States that does not charge admission, the area's economy would suffer greatly. Santa Claus, Indiana, has a slightly larger population of 2,463 residents. There would be no Santa Claus, Indiana, without the economic impact of Holiday World.

Orlando is an anomaly in this discussion. It has become a large urban area, but only because of the theme park industry. Before Mickey arrived in central Florida, Orlando was a small farming town. Today, Orlando has 277,173 residents that would have no reason to live there if it weren't for the economic structure supported by theme parks.

Walt Disney World Resort is the largest single-site employer in the United States. 74,000 cast members work somewhere in the resort. Universal Studios Orlando employs 12,000 people at its three parks and hotels. But the theme park industry is supporting a large secondary market. The Orlando Regional Healthcare System employs 12,754 professionals, and an additional 14,225 people work for Florida Hospital. These healthcare providers would have no reason to exist in Orlando without the fact that people live there to work in the parks. Plus, all of the theme park and healthcare employees have to buy groceries and gas. They have children who need to go to school. These families need homes, utilities, transportation, clothing, and dishwasher repair. As an industry, theme parks support a lot of people in Florida.

During the late 1980s, Disney announced that they were looking to build a theme park in Europe. Cities from all over the continent clamored to be considered. All sorts of creative ideas were implemented with the hope that Mickey would built in a specific country. France was relentless and ultimately provided the best package to Disney.

France has a reputation for being extremely protective of their culture. Then why was this country so eager to import an American theme park? The answer is so simple: economics. Disneyland Paris Resort employs 15,000 people. It's the largest single-site employer in France. For every job at Disneyland Paris, three jobs are created in the supporting hotel, restaurant, and service industries. Disneyland Paris uses just over 3,000 outside suppliers in France. Last year, the resort spent 13.7 billion euros on its supplies. According to a 2012 study conducted by the French government, Disneyland Paris generated fifty billion euros of added value to the French economy during its first twenty years of existence.

I understand that a lot of the numbers in this section are just plain boring. Hopefully not so boring for someone who feeds his or her family from a theme park paycheck. I think it's great that many people make their livelihoods from an industry based upon the principles of providing fun for others. It sure beats the hell out of working in an unsafe ammunition factory for fifteen hours each day.

Dreamlly's
Theme Park Recommendation

Dollywood
Pigeon Forge, Tennessee

Finally, after all these pages, I get to discuss my beloved Dollywood. This will be a short description, but you can read more in my guidebook *Dollywood and Beyond!* The guidebook includes information about all there is to do and see in the Smoky Mountain tourist region. It's updated regularly and available from Amazon.com.

Dollywood is located in the foothills of the Smoky Mountains, just eight miles from Great Smoky Mountains National Park. It's a gorgeous area, with mountains, flowing streams, diverse wildlife, abundant flowers—but what it doesn't have are lots of opportunities for its people. Historically, this is one of the poorest areas of the country. Without the modern tourism industry, most people would have left this region.

At her two theme parks, resort, and two dinner shows, Dolly

Parton directly employs 4,000 people. This is not counting all those that work for the area's hotels, restaurants, and entertainment attractions. Without Dollywood and its 3.5 million yearly visitors, there would not be a need for any of these auxiliary businesses. (Not to mention that the employees of Dollywood use their paychecks to buy groceries, gas, and lots of pancakes.)

Dollywood is a giant love letter from one woman to the community that nurtured her. When you enter the park on Showstreet, you'll instantly see that music is the central theme here. The Showstreet Palace Theater is a fully-functional theater that is capable of handling large sets. In fact, Dollywood has three theaters that can each present Broadway-caliber shows. (In technical terms, this means that Dollywood's three large theaters have enough fly space to accommodate full-size buildings. They also have the equipment to raise and lower those buildings into place.) Dollywood could actually host three touring Broadway shows at one time—no other theme park on the planet, not even Disney, can make this boast.

The lavish theatrical shows are not the only live music you'll experience at Dollywood. There are several smaller venues around the park that offer various types of music all day long. It would be hard for any other theme park to find enough talent to fill all these spaces, but Dolly Parton sort of has some connections in this area. Not only is she a country music star, movie star, and winner of a bazillion awards, but she's also the matriarch of a very large musical family.

The brilliant business minds of Dolly and her partners have been quite strategic in planning for Dollywood's future. They have invested heavily in major coasters to attract those that are maybe too young to even have heard a Dolly Parton song. Dollywood contains Lightning Rod, the world's fastest wooden roller coaster. That's right—here among the slow-cooked brisket and hand-dipped candles is this marvel of design and technology.

Wild Eagle, the nation's first inverted winged coaster, is also at home inside Dollywood. This is just the beginning of Dollywood's impressive coaster collection. To see these coasters gracefully rise above the majestic foothills is a sight to behold.

My favorite attraction in the park is the Dollywood Express. This steam locomotive pulls guests up into the foothills several times each day. (It actually leaves the park for most of its journey.) The Dollywood Express runs on hand-shoveled coal—just as it has since the days of yore. The views of Mt. LeConte from the train are worth the admission price into the park.

Dollywood's grist mill still grinds its own flour using the power of a mountain stream. The flour is baked into all sorts of wonderful creations. In Craftsman's Valley, guests can watch artisans make various items that are as useful as they are beautiful. A real blacksmith bends metal as a woodcarver creates a set of dishes. Glass blowers sit in front of large furnaces and turn sand into works of art. The stoneware produced by Dollywood's potters will last a lifetime.

For those that come to Dollywood because they love Dolly Parton, there is the Chasing Rainbows museum. This large museum uses modern technology to tell Dolly's amazing rags-to-riches story. You'll see many artifacts of her storied career, along with hundreds of awards from around the globe. Of course, no Dolly Parton museum would be complete without displaying her sparkling gowns and tall shoes.

Also on the property is Dollywood's Splash Country. This themed water park is simply stunning, as it makes use of its natural landscape. The waterslides use the foothills for their support, and the lazy river winds through the park like a natural mountain stream. A full-service luxury hotel, Dollywood's DreamMore Resort, completes the property. There are aggressive plans to add another resort and an indoor themed area in the near future.

All of this is amazing. But what makes Dollywood special among theme parks is its philosophy of philanthropy. Dolly's personal desire to give back most of what she has been fortunate enough to earn is quite evident in the park. A portion of all Dollywood receipts goes to Dolly Parton's Imagination Library. This program sends one book each month to children from birth to age five. The program sends out over one million books each month to kids in the US and throughout the English-speaking world. The Dollywood Foundation, another recipient of your theme park dollars, operates too many charities to mention them all. Everything from support for families in need to college scholarships is covered by the foundation. Lastly, Dollywood operates the American Eagle Foundation. Right inside the park, you can visit the world's largest sanctuary for non-releasable birds of prey.

Yes, you do have to pay to enter Dollywood. It also costs money to purchase food and items from the shops. However, a lot of that money finds its way back into the Smoky Mountain region. In fact, if your own town participates in the Imagination Library, some of that money is even finding its way back to you.

Reason #24:

Humans need the anticipation that theme parks foster.

Ebenezer Scrooge is one of the best characters in all of literature. He's just such a complicated person—he's the victim of his own choices. We all love to hate his cranky stinginess, but we also delight in his ultimate transformation.

I spend a lot of time thinking about Scrooge. Probably more time than a mentally healthy person should. I think it's terrifying how easy it would be to become Ebenezer Scrooge. We've all faced hardships in our youth. Most of us know what it's like to not be invited to a birthday party. Any one of us could be just as desperate as Scrooge to hold onto money if we were given the chance.

But of all the sadness involved in Ebenezer's life, the worst is that he has absolutely nothing to look forward to. He certainly never travels. Scrooge doesn't seem like the type to head across the Channel to the French Riviera and hang out on the beach. From the book, we know that he eats the same bowl of crap every single day. He doesn't even have food to look forward to.

Perhaps there is that one day every year when Ebenezer

finds it necessary to purchase a new pair of socks. That must be one hell of a day for him. During the other 364 days, nothing ever changes. Even the weather has little impact on his fashion choices. I doubt he has one of those "I heart London" hats lying around. He doesn't have Christmas to look forward to. Scrooge has absolutely nothing in his future that will make one day even a little bit different from the next. This is not healthy.

Winter gets a little long in Minnesota. I actually don't mind the snow one bit, and even the cold is somewhat exhilarating. But it's dark. We don't see the sun a lot during these months. Even I, the Dolly Parton-loving, Disney-adoring optimist, get down from time to time. But I know there are theme parks ahead of me.

The very best gifts you can give children for the holidays are theme park tickets. Not only are they easy to wrap, but they come with a winter of dreams attached. The kids will know that you are committed to bringing them to the park. They will have months to research the attractions and daydream about the upcoming day. And as an added benefit, you won't have to go to the mall or a big box store. You can purchase theme park tickets online. Most parks have special holiday cards that you can print off to put the tickets in. (If you purchase Dollywood tickets for the holidays, you can download a card of Dolly Parton in a Santa suit.) Some theme parks even have Black Friday deals!

We hear a lot about living in the present. I understand what proponents of that philosophy are attempting to portray: We should live in the moment so that we don't waste time worrying. I agree that it's important to focus on what's happening right now. But what if what's happening right now is a kidney stone? Or an annoying meeting? Or a dreary day? That's when you need to forget about the present and think about something you're looking forward to.

I wish I could take Ebenezer Scrooge to Disneyland Paris. Sure, his head would explode when he saw the price of a T-shirt, but he'd have a blast watching the Pirates of the Caribbean steal all those gold coins. I'd also take him for a journey through the Phantom Manor, Disneyland Paris's version of the Haunted Mansion—Scrooge loves dealing with ghosts and all. I'd try really hard, though, to avoid Scrooge McDuck. I wouldn't want to have to explain that to him.

If I could give Ebenezer something to look forward to, then perhaps he'd let Bob Cratchit have that extra piece of coal.

Dreamlly's **Theme Park Recommendation**

DreamWorld
Gold Coast, Australia

You may anticipate a visit to your local theme park a day or two before you visit, maybe for even a few weeks. But if you have to travel any distance to get to a theme park, your anticipation period will be longer. For most of us, a journey to Australia requires a lot of planning and a trip halfway around the world. It's quite possible to spend years anticipating a visit to Australia.

Australia is a huge country. But luckily for theme park lovers, all of Australia's major theme parks are located within minutes of each other on the Gold Coast. The Gold Coast is a ten hour-drive north of Sydney or an hour south of Brisbane. This is Australia's version of Waikiki, with beach shops and restaurants galore. The beaches here are some of the best in the world, with the beach at Surfer's Paradise being the most popular.

DreamWorld is the largest theme park in Australia. It opened in 1981 after several years of planning and construction. Early executives of the park hired some Imagineers away from Disney. You will definitely notice the influence of Disneyland when you enter the park through Main Street. In fact, a photograph of the entrance to DreamWorld may require multiple glances before you realize that it's not Disneyland.

It's not just the front entrance—many areas of DreamWorld often appear as a sort of bizarro Disneyland. Instead of Mickey Mouse, DreamWorld has Kenny Koala. His girlfriend is Belinda Brown—she's also a koala. (Remember, there is an unwritten theme park rule prohibiting cross-species dating.) And just like at Disneyland, the only actual ride on Main Street is the DreamWorld Railway.

DreamWorld is famous for promoting its Big 9. The Big 9 are a collection of extreme thrill rides, all found within the park. Guests can even choose from various Big 9-themed merchandise items. The Big 9 is comprised of Buzzsaw (tallest inversion ride in the southern hemisphere), Hot Wheels SideWinder (looping high-speed coaster themed after the toy cars), Mick Doohan Motocoaster (motorcycle-themed coaster), Pandamonium (choose your own intensity on this spinning attraction), Tailspin (out-of-control flying ride), the Claw (out-of-control pendulum ride), the Giant Drop (390-foot drop tower), Tower of Terror II (390-foot insane launch coaster), and Wipeout (inverting extreme swing ride).

There are two children's areas in the park. Wiggles World is a themed zone for young kids. It's all based around Australia's superstar group, the Wiggles. DreamWorks Experience is for older children. This land includes attractions based on *Shrek*, *Madagascar,* and *Kung Fu Panda.* There are several well-themed rides in this area.

The most unique area of the park, and my favorite, is DreamWorld Corroboree. This large land is home to over eight hundred animals, all exhibited in their natural habitats. (Yes, real animals—not animatronics. Did I mention that DreamWorld is also one of the largest zoos in Australia?) DreamWorld Corroboree is the place to see pythons, crocodiles, emus, wombats, a whole lot of snakes that can kill you, adorable dingos that can kill you, and shingle-backs (I'm not sure what they are, but they will probably kill you). Of course, there are lots of kangaroos. Really, there are a lot of kangaroos. Seriously—many kangaroos.

Most visitors to the Corroboree spend the majority of their time in Koala Country. This is a land of cuteness overload. It's quite amazing, and you'll find that an hour or two simply flies by in this land. For an extra fee, guests can cuddle a koala and have their photograph taken. Also, just in case you didn't see them in the other section of the Corroboree, there are lots of kangaroos in Koala Country.

Before you leave DreamWorld Corroboree, you must visit the cassowaries. A cassowary is part bird and part Satan. Its appearance is so strange that just looking at it might kill you. In fact, the cassowary is the deadliest bird on Earth. They can run super-fast, they swim super-fast, and they have five-inch-long daggers attached to their feet. As if that weren't enough, cassowaries have this weird flat horn on their heads that can kill anything with one bonk. Fortunately, these birds make a warning sound before they attack. Unfortunately, the sound is the lowest-frequency birdcall known and is not able to be heard by human ears.

There is really no reason why I wrote so much about

cassowaries. It's just that they're so interesting and I never would have learned about them if I hadn't gone to DreamWorld. There are a lot of things I would never have learned if I didn't visit theme parks.

DreamWorld has a water park next door called WhiteWater World. WhiteWater World is included in the price of DreamWorld admission. DreamWorld does not operate any of its own hotels, but there are many hotels in the area with great beach amenities.

There are a few things you need to remember. For those of you reading this in the US and Europe, remember that Australia's seasons are opposite to ours. Summer is December through March. Also, please remember to wear plenty of sunscreen while visiting DreamWorld. In the southern hemisphere, the sun gets hotter the further north you travel. DreamWorld is considerably more northern than Sydney, and the sun is intense. You've anticipated visiting Australia for years—don't ruin it by ignoring the sun.

Reason #25:

Healthy humans have fun and can discover it inside a theme park.

Open your web browser and Google "Why do we need to have fun?" You'll get links to a whole lot of articles about the human need for fun. Some researchers say that people who have fun are less likely to be sick. Others say that fun will make you more productive. Whatever. I detest these articles. If you need to have fun in order to be more productive, then you are missing the entire point.

You need fun because it's fun. End of story. Literally.

Dreamlly's Theme Park Recommendation

Story Mountain
Sartell, Minnesota

Theme park people are dreamers. I've saved Story Mountain for last because it's a dream—and that makes it the best theme park of all. I've visited Story Mountain many times over the years—it's never crowded.

Story Mountain is located in Sartell, Minnesota. Sartell is a lovely town on the Mississippi about two hours northwest of Minneapolis. In 1905, a paper mill was founded on the banks of the river in Sartell. This mill grew, over the next hundred years, into the largest manufacturer of glossy magazine paper in the world. Unfortunately, the digital revolution was not good for Sartell. As magazine readership plunged, so did the need for magazine paper. After a disastrous fire in 2012, the paper mill never reopened. Sartell lost a lot of good jobs and its place on the map—this beautiful river town lost its identity. Then, Story Mountain opened, and things got better.

The former mill site along the river is the perfect location for Story Mountain. Not only does the theme park offer stunning views of the river, but it also provides much-needed employment for the people of central Minnesota. The original paper mill dam and bridge are cleverly used in the design of the park. Guests can access the pedestrian bridge and walking trails without paying for admission.

Story Mountain is dedicated to the power of storytelling. Though inspired by Disneyland, this theme park has a charm all its own. Guests enter through the moderately priced, but well-themed, Library Hotel. Here, rooms are categorized according to the Dewey Decimal system. For example, the seventh floor is dedicated to the arts. Specifically, room 780 is themed for music biographies, with portraits of Mozart and Beethoven hanging on the walls. (Room 364 is quite graphic and reserved for adults only.)

After passing through the Library Hotel, you'll enter American Tale Avenue. Here, you can shop at P. Bunyan's Mercantile and grab a snack at Johnny Appleseed's Bakery. You may also visit John Henry's T-shirt Emporium and Calamity Jane's Assorted Sundries. For those of you traveling with pets, they can be boarded at Babe's Blue Adventure—a full-service kennel located inside the park.

At the end of American Tale Avenue, guests can meander around the beautiful Genre Gardens. This is where fans of the Story Mountain mascots can meet their favorite character and have a photograph taken. You might see Dreamlly the narwhal and his best friend Sinclair. Sinclair is also a narwhal. (FYI—Dreamlly is blue and Sinclair is green. There is an urban legend that Dreamlly and Sinclair are dating, but Story Mountain has not confirmed this.) Genre Gardens is also the place to meet Buffy the beluga and her crazy little penguin friend called PoPo. During select times of the year, guests can meet Ms. Prancy Pants—she is a sassy reindeer that is the symbol of Story Mountain's Yuletale Extravaganza.

Directly at the end of American Tale Avenue and behind Genre

Gardens is the massive Sea of Words. This body of water forms the central portion of the park and provides a space for Story Mountain's elaborate water spectaculars. The water for the Sea of Words is pumped directly from the Mississippi River. After running through the park, this water is returned to the river cleaner than when it was removed. (Note: Narwhals play a starring role in all of Story Mountain's water shows. However, even though they appear quite realistic, all the narwhals in the park are animatronic marvels of technology. No real narwhal, nor real narwhal horn, will ever appear at Story Mountain. Of course, there are lots of light-up plastic horns that guests can buy, as well as the famous Dreamlly hats that have a cloth narwhal horn protruding from the front.)

Around the perimeter of the Sea of Words, guests can choose their own adventure by journeying through Story Mountain's themed lands. At first glance, Mystery Cove looks like a typical New England seaside village. But this is a land of unexpected homicides and missing paintings. Here, you can take a ride on Agatha Christie's Train to Nowhere or wander the streets of London as you explore the interactive attraction Sherlock's Secrets.

As you exit Mystery Cove and cross a foggy stream, you'll see the strange formations of Creepy Isle. Every day is October 31 on this island. As soon as you enter, you'll hear the screaming from Creepy Isle's two massive roller coasters, Dracula's Flight and Mr. Hyde's Revenge. The Haunted Bookshelf is a dark ride through the pages of literature's finest horror stories. Creepy Isle is also the location of the large Théâtre de Cauchemar. This theater presents a live forty-five minute musical based on *Buffy, the Vampire Slayer*. Of course, the tallest attraction on Creepy Isle is the 450-foot Phantom's Drop. On this drop tower, guests sit in a massive chandelier that rises to the top and then plummets down to the strains of Verdi's *Rigoletto*.

Fairytale Village makes a nice contrast to Creepy Isle. This is the land for children of all ages to ride through their favorite stories. (This land is carefully crafted to avoid the attention of a certain mouse and his teams of lawyers.) A short-cut through Romance Lane brings guests to Biography Square. Here, you can watch the animatronic spectacular inside the Hall of Winners of the Nobel Prize for Literature. This spectacle is narrated by Sinclair Lewis, the first American to win the prestigious prize.

The most extreme coasters in the park can be found in Sci-Fi City. Sci-Fi City includes the amazing Hitchhiker's Ride to the Galaxy and the vomit-inducing War of the Whirls. Older teens and adults may want to brave the oddness of Sci-Fi City's Dystopian Dome. It's always 1984 inside this extreme attraction.

Another shortcut (that's unusually long), Fantasy Fairway, brings guests to the Adventure Exploratory. Fantasy Fairway is a winding path with lots of obstacles along the way. Adventure Exploratory is where you can experience simulated earthquakes, tornados, and tsunamis.

Adventure Exploratory contains the entrance to Story Mountain's Waters of History. Inside this water park, you can explore the fact and fiction of historical tales. Try to dodge sprays of water in the Battlefield Wave Pool. Ride through pyramids, temples, and chariots on the Slides of the Ancients. Or lazily float past masterpieces on the Renaissance Rafts.

Food is available all over Story Mountain. Inside Great Expectations Buffet, guests can choose from selections mentioned in the work of Charles Dickens. (Some of it is kind of disgusting.) In the James Michener Café, the food seems overembellished, but it's so good that the guests eat it anyway. Adventure

Exploratory offers meat that is often undercooked, but since it's hard to come by, you'll enjoy it nonetheless.

The most popular place to eat in the park is Roald Dahl's Factory of Chocolate, Peaches, and Manners. All sorts of wonderful high-calorie creations are available at this colorful establishment. However, children should be advised to be on their best behavior. Good kids are rewarded with extra chocolate. Bad kids will find that their seats are spring-loaded; at the touch of a button, bad kids are ejected through holes in the roof and eventually land in the parking lot.

Behind all of this is the towering and iconic symbol of the park: the Mountain of Moments. From a distance, it looks like a mountain made of stone with several peaks and craggy valleys. But as you approach, you will see that the entire mountain is made from the sculpted forms of great moments in literature. Look closely, and you'll see Ebenezer Scrooge and the Ghost of Christmas Present as they observe the Cratchit family at their meager table. On another surface, you'll see Anne Shirley riding in a carriage with Matthew and Marilla. You can find Romeo and Juliet as they are secretly married. The Joad family and their overpacked car form one of the base supports for the mountain. Max and a few Wild Things form one of the peaks. Odysseus is somewhere on the mountain, as are Quasimodo, Harry Potter, Mrs. Frisby, Hester Prynne, and Gustav von Aschenbach. On the top of the mountain, you can spot a simple raven. And if you look just right, when the sun is setting, you'll see Charlotte and her radiant web.

Story Mountain is a beautiful place that you can visit anytime you want. Just close your eyes, and there it is! (Really, you should visit now because it's rather inexpensive. If, by some miracle, I ever do build Story Mountain—it won't be free.) Yes, Story

Mountain is a fantasy that exists in my head. Does that make it any less real? Not for me. You should construct your own Story Mountain that you can visit when life gets just a little too real for you.

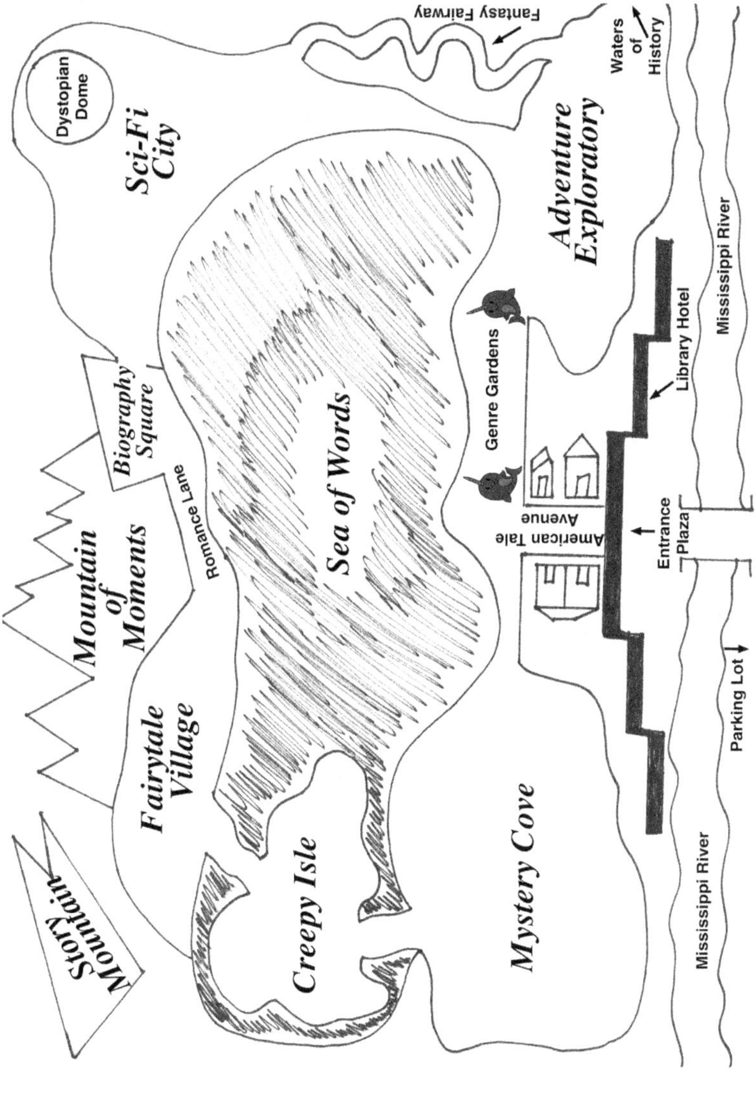
Story Mountain
Mountain of Moments
Fairytale Village
Biography Square
Romance Lane
Sci-Fi City
Dystopian Dome
Fantasy Fairway
Waters of History
Adventure Exploratory
Sea of Words
Creepy Isle
Mystery Cove
Genre Gardens
American Tale Avenue
Entrance Plaza
Library Hotel
Parking Lot
Mississippi River
Mississippi River

Conclusion

That's it—twenty-five reasons why theme parks are modern shrines. By this point, you're probably so tired of listening to me going on and on that you're ready to throw yourself off the highest roller coaster you can find. Just make sure to fasten your seat belt first.

In millions of years, our civilization may be buried under layers of rock. I hope that when future archeologists dig up our stuff, they find Disneyland instead of Dachau. I want them to discover a carousel before they uncover a prison. I hope they find theme parks and not battlefields.

It's time for me to say goodbye and for you to get yourself to a theme park. And in the great theme park of life, I hope you spend a lot more time on the rides than you do waiting in line.

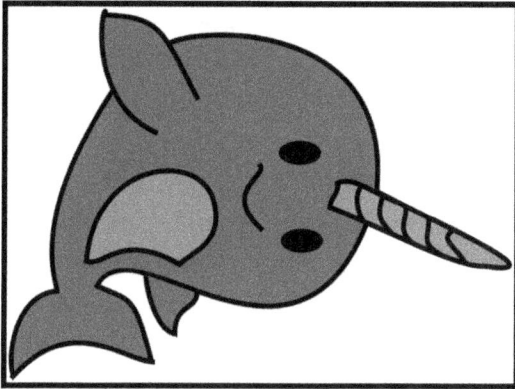

All I Really Needed to Know I Learned in Theme Parks

- A good map is essential to find your way.
- If you want to eat dinner, you can't spend all of your money on games.
- Waiting in line is dull, but it gets better if you can occupy your own brain for a while.
- Respecting other people's space is a good thing to do.
- Facing a fear can be extremely difficult, but the reward is amazing.
- You may be disappointed at times. Just deal with it.
- Like the weather, things will happen that you can't control. Just deal with it.
- Planning ahead makes your day a lot easier.
- Keep track of your stuff because nobody else will.
- Prioritize what you want to do, and make choices that lead in that direction.
- Taking care of your body is important if you want to fit on all the rides.
- If your group splits up, always make a plan to find each other again.

- Cleanliness is a good thing, and if you keep things clean, others will too.
- An active fantasy life inspires you to make your real life even better.
- Creativity still means something on this planet.
- A healthy human always has something to look forward to.
- Be nice to all those who are doing their jobs because tomorrow that will be you.
- As you get older, sitting on a bench and watching a roller coaster can be as much fun as riding it yourself.
- Laughter and having fun are essential parts of life worthy of your time and money.

www.ingramcontent.com/pod-product-compliance
Lightning Source LLC
LaVergne TN
LVHW051629080426
835511LV00016B/2255